From Rags to Ricky

Also by Sid Owen

Life on a Plate: The Journey of an Unlikely Chef

From Rags to Ricky

Sid Owen

with Martin Gray

MACMILLAN

First published 2021 by Macmillan
an imprint of Pan Macmillan
The Smithson, 6 Briset Street, London EC1M 5NR
EU representative: Macmillan Publishers Ireland Ltd, 1st Floor,
The Liffey Trust Centre, 117–126 Sheriff Street Upper,
Dublin 1, D01 YC43
Associated companies throughout the world
www.panmacmillan.com

ISBN 978-1-5290-0841-8

1 3 5 7 9 8 6 4 2

A CIP catalogue record for this book is available from the British Library.

Typeset by Palimpsest Book Production Ltd, Falkirk, Stirlingshire
Printed and bound by CPI Group (UK) Ltd, Croydon, CR0 4YY

Visit **www.panmacmillan.com** to read more about all our books
and to buy them. You will also find features, author interviews and
news of any author events, and you can sign up for e-newsletters
so that you're always first to hear about our new releases.

For Mum

Prologue

THE PLANE LOOKED MASSIVE AS I WALKED ACROSS THE tarmac at Luton Airport, Mum holding my hand to make sure I didn't dart off. Dad and my brothers climbed easily up the clanging metal stairs while my little legs struggled to keep up. No way was I being left behind. For the first time ever, we were all getting a proper family holiday abroad, in sunny Minorca. We'd seen the posters on travel agents' windows, all palm trees and beaches, that had been the nearest we'd ever got to visiting anywhere different, but now we were actually going ourselves. This was going to be sweet. Everyone was fit to bursting.

It only took us kids seconds to work out that if you pressed a button, the seat reclined. And if you stood up on it you could reach a light switch you could flick on and off. Basically anything within reach that could be played with was played with to maximum effect before Mum or Dad delivered a slap. Everyone liked the seat pocket in front, with all magazines and stuff, but best of all, there was a foldaway table. My older brothers remember being even more excited when Mum said we'd get a tray of food with pudding and everything once we were in the sky. Then this beautiful woman in a fancy uniform was smiling down at us and checking seat belts while another one did a safety demo, which looked like some sort of strange arm dance.

Anyway, there we are, on the tarmac, about to taxi down the runway and take off. Mum, Dad, Mark, Darren, Scott and me. The crew had just started shutting the doors and pulling the stairs away when police cars suddenly appeared outside the window, all flashing lights and sirens, getting closer and closer. Next thing we knew, the cabin was full of the Old Bill, barrelling up the aisle towards us. They grabbed my dad, stuck him in handcuffs and dragged him out. We were screaming, terrified. Then they marched Mum, my brothers and me off the plane and drove us all away in the back of a van, or 'meat wagon' as my family called them.

What happened next is a blank in my memory. We must have been taken back to London. I don't know what Dad was arrested for – but they didn't manage to nail him that time. It would have been better for us all if they had.

1

Steak and Kidney Sidney

MY MUM'S LIFE HAD SEEN A FAIR BIT OF DRAMA, MOSTLY related to her choice in men, by the time I came along.

I was born in January 1972 in the Royal Free Hospital, Islington, north London. These days you think of Islington as a wealthy area but it wasn't back then. We lived to the north of Pentonville, part of a large working-class population which was usually at the sharp end of any economic crisis. I arrived right at the start of one of them. Britain was soon to be in total financial meltdown. The national debt was so bad that the whole country was on the brink of bankruptcy. Industrial relations were in tatters, with my early childhood marked by constant strikes, three-day weeks and regular power cuts, sometimes no electricity at all.

My family had been hit by many slumps down the generations. My maternal grandfather, Donald MacNeil, who, as you might have guessed, was Scottish, was born in the early 1900s and had battled through the Great Depression of the 1930s. Forced to come down to London to try to find work, he arrived without two bob to rub together, but rolled up his sleeves and grafted away at whatever he could. It was far from rich pickings back then, but he was canny and managed to get himself one of the best newspaper pitches in the City. It was not that far from Pentonville geographically, but, as the financial centre of the country, was a different world. Grandpa ran a tight stand, but actually selling the newspapers was only a part of it. They say he was also great with people, genuinely liked them. He was as working class as they come but could charm the pants off the toffs. He had the banter. The wit. The warmth. It was the same then as it is now. If you put a bit of sparkle into someone's day, make them laugh even for a moment, they walk away with a smile, feeling a bit better about the world and themselves. It's a kind of acting, a well-crafted routine. Happy customers would then come back and hopefully be more generous with their tips. Donald also needed to make the right friends and avoid the wrong enemies because if you didn't, your little earner would soon be someone else's.

My granny Florence was a Londoner and quite a character herself. Known to everyone as Flo, she was a bit older than Donald, having been born at the end of Queen Victoria's reign. I wonder how many pubs were already

4

called 'The Queen Vic' back then. Granny had been married once before, with four children, by the time she met Donald. The oldest was Florence, who everyone called Flossie, so as not to confuse her with her mum. No one born Florence seemed actually to be called Florence back then. Then came William, known as Billy – as no one seemed to be called William either – then June, or 'Junie'. Finally there was Evelyn, who was adopted towards the start of the Second World War when Granny Flo had already turned forty.

Donald and Flo were both already well established in the community when they met. Flo was a force of nature with an entrepreneurial side. She was very well connected and respected but not to be messed with. During the war and for years afterwards many goods were rationed and in short supply and Granny seemed to have a network that could lay their hands on what people wanted – and also deal with problems, so you could go to her for pretty much anything, from black-market stockings to calming down trouble and sorting issues.

I don't know what happened to Granny's husband but at some point she met Donald, who'd been a bachelor till then, and he fell for Flo. They married in the early 1940s and moved in together into a medium-sized terrace house on Baron Street, Islington, with Flo's children, then had two of their own. My mum Joan was born in 1944 bang in the middle of what people called 'the Baby Blitz', the German bombing raids that targeted south-east England. More and more buildings were reduced to rubble every night, with a growing death toll of those inside or on the streets who didn't make it to the shelters in time. 'Joanie', as Mum was known pretty much from the word go, was a beautiful, loving, feisty and funny little girl. A ray of sunshine in dark times and the absolute apple of her daddy's eye. My Aunt Carol came along a year later in 1945, just at the end of the war. So there they were, all eight of them, crammed into what seemed like a happy if chaotic home.

Because of their noses for business and determination to graft, Flo and Donald had done well for themselves for a working-class couple who'd started with nothing. There were a lot of mouths to feed, though, and the whole of Britain was thrown into a post-war economic crisis, so money could never be taken for granted. Much of Islington had been bombed to within an inch of its life with a tragic loss of life. Their house survived the war but was bulldozed later anyway, and they got a council flat.

I never got a chance to talk to Mum about her life growing up or what dreams she might have had when she was a teenager. Probably she didn't think beyond getting a job to help pay the bills and going out on a Saturday night. By the time she was sixteen, the long dreary post-war era must have felt like it might be finally ending. Coffee bars had sprung up over the city, places for teenagers to meet alongside the local dance halls. I can imagine Mum being chatted up by young men in sharp suits and maybe even with their own transport. Guys who could flash the cash, make a girl laugh and feel like a princess. There may have been precious little actual glamour in working-class Islington, with its grubby streets and bomb sites, but my mum was a really pretty girl who could make herself look glamorous and see where it got her. No doubt she was streetwise in some ways, but she was also too innocent in others, and where that got her was pregnant at seventeen by a handsome charmer from Kentish Town.

When my eldest brother Mark arrived in 1962, however, she was totally bowled over with love for her beautiful baby boy. Everything about Mark's dad was, and remains, a mystery. Mum didn't talk about him, and he was out of the picture long before Mark was born.

So there was my mum, still only in her teens, with a baby boy and the father nowhere to be seen. When those are the cards you've been dealt, I suppose you do what you can to stay strong and make the most of it. She was totally devoted to Mark but she was trapped, lonely and still very young, though feisty, funny and pretty as ever. It was unlikely a young librarian would sweep her off her feet. Not that she'd have wanted one if he tried.

When Mark was four, Mum met a new man, Dave, and they had two children: Darren, who was born in 1968, and Scott in 1969. It was almost like a normal household for a while, with Darren and Scott's dad acting like a regular father, apart from the fact that he didn't exactly have a regular job.

His main area of endeavour was robbing post office

vehicles. He had a system that seemed to get results back in the day – though it wouldn't work now, with all the computerization and security cameras. The rewards weren't huge but the risks were relatively low. He'd grab bags of mail and root around inside, looking for new family allowance books that were common back then (family allowance was what came before child benefit and you had to have a little book to go and claim it). He'd then get hold of his mum, sisters-in-law and friends of my mum and hand them a bundle each. They would go round post offices all over London cashing them up. Nothing local, obviously – too risky. They'd divvy up the money, then everyone got fed.

This attempt at happy families all came to an abrupt halt when Dave took a risk too far and got caught doing a proper bank job. He was arrested and sentenced at the Old Bailey. Twenty-one years for armed robbery.

Now, twenty-one years is a long time in anyone's book, so my mum just sort of went 'See you later'. And then she met my dad. She jumped right out of the frying pan into the fire, though, because my dad was an armed robber as well. This was the life she knew. These were her peers, her whole world. I don't think she'd have known how to escape it even if she wanted to, so instead she kept getting involved.

Mum had managed to get jobs in pubs and the bingo hall at Chapel Market. She was great at both as she was the real life and soul of any room. Always very pretty with a big personality. It's a tough gig being on your own with three young kids, though. Neighbours and family would help out in the evenings if Mum was working.

By the time I came along as the baby brother, by the third dad, we were living at Mandeville Houses on Mantell Street, the first social housing estate in the area to be built by the local council rather than by a trust. Finished in 1930, it was a big old place five storeys high. Everything seems huge when you're a little kid, but these flats weren't. You opened the front door into a narrow passage with small rooms on either side. There was a tiny kitchen and bathroom. When Mandeville was built, though, an inside bathroom, not a toilet shared with the neighbours and a tub in the kitchen, was a real luxury.

There must have been enough dodgy money coming in from somewhere, as Mum and Dad had obviously splashed out on the décor. We had a particularly swirly carpet in fetching shades of golden brown, mustardy brown, dark brown and red. We also briefly had a fashionable shag pile carpet, which was like walking over woolly un-mown grass. If grass was the colour of Colman's mustard. A lot of things in the 1970s came in weird shades of brown and gold. Even the cars. A long shaggy carpet may have been the least practical thing possible to have in a small front room with four growing boys, and after about a week it was in a sorry state. All flattened out and kind of greasy to touch.

We also had a velour three-piece suite and a 'feature

fireplace' – basically a two-bar electric heater with lots of moulded plastic in the shape of logs and flames which were lit up by a bulb. It wasn't very convincing but I loved it. Lying by that reddish glow, feeling the heat from those bars was my favourite place in the room. Unfortunately it was also all my brothers' favourite place, so me being the youngest I usually lost that fight.

There was also a 'music centre', which was mum's pride and joy. It contained a turntable (or record player, as people said back then) a cassette player and a radio. The sound was pretty good when it was working – but more on that later.

Even though we were right on the edge of bustling, energetic Chapel Market, Mandeville was like a self-contained world. It loomed over all the older low-rise buildings around it – though it was not as high as the nearby council estates built in the 1960s and 1970s. You entered the estate through an arched tunnel in the building that led into a central courtyard where there were lines and lines of doorways to the stairwells leading up to all the flats. If you shouted upwards in the tunnel you could get a bit of a scary echo off it as the sound bounced back. We lived just by the archway. Mandeville had well over a hundred flats, so although you knew all your neighbours you were closest to the ones who shared your stairwell. It seemed in our childhood world that it didn't matter where we went, we'd know someone.

The estate was what you might call 'self-policing'. The actual police were definitely not welcome inside, though we saw loads of Old Bill come in and grab people. I remember seeing a cop car abandoned there. They must have come in and given up, or been beaten up or something. The community had their own honour code though, and while anyone who crossed the line wouldn't have been scared of the police, they were terrified of the self-policing. You knew, even as a little 'un, that grassing anyone up to the Old Bill was one of the most serious offences everywhere on the estate, but especially in our family.

If anything happened, the word would spread like wild-fire. Any stranger coming into the estate would be spotted, noted, stared at and, if they were young and male, could be in trouble very soon. One day we heard a massive bang from the Chapel Street end of the estate and everyone rushed out. The council were drilling the road and one poor sod's drill had gone straight through the mains electricity cable, which exploded. He was standing there, not a stitch on. Enough voltage to power the whole estate went up his pneumatic drill and right through him. All us kids were out there staring at this guy who was literally smoking, burned from top to bottom, and shaking like crazy. I can still remember the smell of frying skin and hair. It was horrible.

Mandeville was known on the outside as being very rough. It was a real old kind of tenement community where no one had a pot to piss in but everyone knew each other and your neighbours became your friends. People would really help each other out and you could just go and ring your neighbour's doorbell if you needed something. Looking back, that was a bit of a lifesaver for my mum.

I was called David after my dad, although everyone knew him as 'Porky'. They say I was a chubby little baby, so I became 'Steak and Kidney Sidney', which immediately got shortened to Sid, and that's what I've been called ever since. Mum found out too late that my dad had two sides, and that the bad side was evil, especially on the drink, when he'd become loud, angry and aggressive. We'd hear him coming in from the pub and instantly everything would feel ominous while we waited to see who he'd pick on. He used to beat Mum up – then he started on us. I remember hiding, scared and worried for my mum. She kept chucking him out because he was just too violent and no way was she going to let someone hurt her boys. Robbing banks was one thing but violence against kids was another.

One time, he accused Darren of some minor misde-meanour, picked him up and hung him out of a window by his ankles. Our flat was a few floors up. Luckily Mum was in the middle of the ironing in the other room, so the second she realized what was happening she ripped the still red-hot iron from its socket, rushed through and threat-ened to burn a hole in his back if he didn't pull Darren in. That was about the last straw. He may have been violent but Mum was well connected and respected by the local underworld, which, as I said before, had its own style of community policing. If she'd have said the word, he'd have been sorted out.

She never made the call, though that time he got a warning. Making that call would have been the last resort. She had her pride, her memories of first falling for him, and thought she could sort it out herself. He kept crawling back, apologising, promising never to do it again. She kept hoping that was true but it never was.

Around that time, we became very good friends with the neighbours living directly below us, Chrissie and Rodney Freed. Mum got on well with them and they would look after us if she was working nights at the pub or bingo hall. Rodney even seemed to be able to handle my dad's temper. When Dad was in a rage and things got rough in our house, I would go downstairs to their flat where it was safe. I was friends with the Freeds' son Jamie, who I used to play with because he was the same age as me. He was probably my best friend when I was really young, before I started school.

Then when I started primary school I made friends who would change my life. I was in the same class as a girl called Joanne Wooder who used to be met by her mum, Maureen, and little brother Danny at the gate. Somehow I struck up a friendship with them and I'd join them when they took Danny to play on the swings in the park. I remember one day he somehow got putty in his hair and Joanne set about trying to remove it. For some reason, after that, I felt that I had to look after him, same as Joanne did. She was my classmate and my friend, and I felt protective of her little brother. It wasn't long before Danny and I became best friends. The Wooders lived down the road on Mathilda Street in an actual house, which was also council at that point.

But I'm getting ahead of myself. Right now it was us in Mandeville Houses, with our neighbours the Freeds. Because the flats were small, we didn't really spend much time indoors. All the kids used to play out in the central courtyard, where we were never out of sight. The mums would also hang out washing there and sit on the wall where the kids were playing. I can remember Mum sitting there, watching us, with Chrissie and other neighbours, just chatting away. You don't get that now.

There was a slide in the courtyard and Jamie and I used to go down it on a bike, which was fun because we'd half lose control as we skidded down. Chrissie would go stark raving mad, frightened we'd hurt ourselves, or hurt someone else. She'd come out and shriek, 'What the fucking hell are you doing?! You don't go down slides on bikes!' We also entertained ourselves by pestering Bobby Bradstock, who had a fruit and veg stall right at the edge of the estate where it met Chapel Market. He used to park his lorry in our bit of the courtyard and let us kids go in. We used to play in it, around it and under it. Bobby would have to check all over before he drove off.

We were out on the streets a lot, especially in any decent weather. I suppose that seems odd now. You don't really see young kids hanging about, playing on inner-city streets any more. I think back in the day, the local attitude was that nothing too bad could happen to kids out of school. It was all pretty safe. We had a good community, everyone knew each other, there was lots of big families. Everyone felt a little bit more community spirited, almost like a family that looked out for each other. Not that the local underworld was exactly pure as the driven snow but one thing was certain: if anyone hurt a local kid they would be hunted down. Nothing the police could do would come anywhere near what would happen to them in the community.

The connected families were able to hold things together. It was old-school gangster style. People wouldn't burgle their neighbours. They had their backs. Some of the shops would get burgled, the big chains, and banks would get robbed. Not on the doorstep though. The community looked after itself and the police didn't get much of a look in.

I stayed very close to the Freeds the whole time we were in Mandeville and afterwards as well, when we were moved out to Stonefield Street. They became like extended family to me and my brothers and were a great source of comfort and security. They were always really loving to their kids. Rodney would cuddle and play fight with Jamie on the sofa but I didn't like being cuddled. I only wanted cuddles from my mum.

The neighbours knew my dad was beating up my mum, my brothers and basically anyone who got within his radius when he lost it. People used to say 'Joanie and Porky was always having battles'. But 'having battles' underplayed the horror of it all. Rodney still tells me, 'Your dad was a proper fucking nut.'

The Freeds used to hear all the screams and think, 'What's Porky fucking done this time?' We'd run away if we could but it was horrible knowing he'd be beating mum up. Sometimes, if we were all there, my brothers and me would try to protect her. I was only tiny but as the others got bigger they could sometimes manage it. He used to have a go at her when my older brothers were out though, or when all of us were out. We'd come home to find Mum all beaten up and crying. Things smashed up all over the shop.

Because Rodney could control Dad, he'd sometimes rush up and check up on us if he was home and heard things kicking off. He thought he'd seen it all but one time even he was totally shocked. He told me that Dad had got his hands on a life-size mannequin and thought it would be funny to dress it in Mum's clothes and one of her wigs then make it look like she was dead in the bath. Rodney came up into the flat when he heard us screaming. I don't remember this but he said I was shaking like a leaf and couldn't speak. He dragged me downstairs to their flat.

I know now that I've blocked out a lot of my dad's behaviour that traumatized me at the time. Some of the most shocking moments only came back when talking to my brothers and other people during the research for this book. The crazy incident at Luton Airport has been kept alive though, as it's so out there; we've laughed about it down the years.

My dad eventually got done for a heavy-duty robbery that was enough to put him away for a long stretch. Everyone was glad to see the back of Porky.

2

Down the Market

IF YOU'D BEEN TO ISLINGTON FOR THE FIRST TIME IN the last twenty years or so, the picture I've been painting probably doesn't seem that familiar. Now, Upper Street, the main street in the area, is fashionable, packed with bars and restaurants and chichi shops. In the seventies and eighties, though, it was rough and ready. And it was dead, too. A lot of the businesses were boarded up and even the flats above the shops had no one living in them. I remember fabric shops and old-fashioned establishments selling industrial-strength underwear to the more mature customer by appointment. There were hairdressers but not trendy ones like you get today – more like blue rinses and a price war to the bottom for the cheapest haircut. A few offices sold car insurance or whatever. One lettings agent, perhaps, in the whole street. Traditional hardware shops. And one or two DHSS places you'd go if you were applying for assistance – what is now called income support.

For us, as kids and teenagers, it was mostly boring, not much to catch the eye from one end of Upper Street to the other, with just one or two exceptions. Like Reckless Records. When we got our own independent record store on Upper Street, that felt exciting. We were like, 'Woohoo, we're coming up in the world!'

A lot of kids, including me, bought their shoes from Jimmy's, which was owned by a Greek family. They had two shops next to each other – Marathon Sports that sold trainers and Jimmy's, selling kids' shoes. Despite the huge changes in Islington, the shop is still there, still owned by the same family and the same assistant who was around when I was a kid, George, still works Saturdays.

There was always someone trying to pull a scam. Like guys trying to buy an odd shoe half-price, claiming they were due to have their leg amputated the following week. It was obvious to everyone they'd stolen a shoe from somewhere else and were trying to make a pair. The chat would go:

'Why do you want one shoe? You've got two legs?'

'I'm having one amputated.'

'Why? You seem fine walking on it now.'

'Oh no – I've terrible problems with my legs . . .'

I remember just up from Jimmy's, at the library, there used to be an old pub with a chess club upstairs. Quite a lot of the homeless guys used to come to the club – I think you got free tea and toast. You had to be playing chess, though. A mate of mine used to go there as a kid, thinking he was doing really well, winning games, and then realized the homeless blokes were happily getting beaten by an eleven-year-old because they were only there for the free tea and toast.

The Business Design Centre on Upper Street used to be 'the Aggie', the Royal Agricultural Hall, though it was a big derelict dump covered in corrugated iron when I was growing up. That was before a local family came to the rescue and bought it in the 1980s. Sam Morris had started with a store in Brick Lane in the East End and become a successful shopfitter. He'd made his pile and retired. Then one day he said, 'I've got to buy the Aggie.' There was talk at the time of knocking it down. He got his family together and told them what he was planning. His kids, who'd been through private school and were grown up by then and comfortable, were pretty nervous about what seemed like a crazy risk. Sam's missus said, 'Look, your dad made the money and if he wants to take the risk on the Aggie you're going to back him.' They did and Sam pulled it off. The Aggie was reborn as the Building Design Centre, which opened in 1986.

Upper Street splits a neighbourhood known as Barnsbury and that was always a wealthier pocket – even then some posh people lived there, in big, beautiful houses. The poshest were the professional types, like lawyers. Maybe some posh arty types – architects, hippie intellectuals, art school tutors. A mate of mine told me a great story that happened back around the 1970s. This was when a few brave, upwardly mobile professional types had started to move in as it was close to the City and you'd get a lot of flat for your money. A young accountant was up early one day, grafting away on a pile of documents at his desk next to the front window overlooking the park. At 6.30 a.m., a van appeared and a few guys in overalls got out and began taking the gates off the park entrance. He was impressed by how quiet they were, obviously not wanting to disturb anyone. He got on with his paperwork, the van drove off and he started thinking, 'They were up awfully early for council maintenance.'

It turned out that the driver was the brother of his neighbour, who was a real old Islington type. A few days later, the neighbour wasn't looking his usual cheery self and the young accountant asked how things were. 'Not so great,' he said. 'My brother's just been nicked for stealing the bloody park gates. We've just arranged a big birthday party for him as well.' The thing went to court, the brother got done and had his birthday in Pentonville.

But for all the upwardly mobile types, there were also loads of scruffy terraces in this area, all split into flats and rented out. A lot of Irish families lived in them. We were told a lot of crap about them being terrorists, as people were really paranoid about the IRA back then. I know someone who said none of his friends would come to visit him in Islington because it was too terrifying to go there in case you got murdered by the terrorists, criminals and crazy people.

There were people from different ethnic backgrounds

and different religions in the community. The way to over-come barriers was by getting to know each other, discovering how much we had in common. When it came down to it, we all liked good food and good music, which was enough for most people.

People got to know each other. If you'd not been paid you could still go out and 'tick' your drinks in the pub or 'tick' your lunch at the local cafe, until you got your money at the end of the month. You could even buy a record or a pair of jeans on tick, paying the week after because the shop owners knew their customers.

The buzz was Chapel Market, to the east of Upper Street, down near Angel tube station. Whatever direction you came from, once you got there, bang, suddenly there was an explosion of life and colour. When you turned off Upper Street, you left behind the shops and offices, the brown and grey buildings and the quieter leafy streets the middle classes already had their eye on, and stepped into bustle and noise. Full on technicolour. All the market traders had different coloured awnings and they were all shouting out to customers to come and see what they had to sell. Everyone talked to you and every bloke got called John – which would cause kids of the same name to start and look around. My mate John, who I didn't know back then, still jokes about. He says it used to confuse the hell out of him, because he thought everyone knew who he was. He lived the other side of Upper Street, in the posher bit, but his godfather used to take him up to Chapel Market and he really did know every trader. They would walk up and down past the stalls then go for jellied eels or pie and mash.

Chapel Street Market is still there but it's not the same. It was a proper working traders' market back then. There were many more stalls crowding the road and not really that many shops. The market was full of people making things happen for themselves. It was exciting, the real colour and flavour of Islington. That was where everyone went to buy their fruit and veg, even the posh people. Back then, it was everyone's first option. People would talk about going 'down Chap' or ask, 'Are you going down Chap?' In the local accent it sounded like d-a-n-c-h-a-p. 'Dan Chap' was where you went to get pretty much anything you needed.

One of the first Marks & Spencers in London was on Chapel Market and there had been a Sainsbury's there since 1882, one of the earliest branches to open after the original shop. There was also a Woolworths, or 'Woolies', as everyone said. For food, there was a Wimpy and M. Manze, which everyone just called Manze's, one of the great pie and mash shops. I've always been into my food and I can still remember the smell that hit me walking in off the street – baking steak and pies and bubbling gravy (called liquor). If you wanted sweets you headed to Franks, while De Marco's sold ice cream. There was even an apple fritters store. Anthony Jackson's had the best broken biscuits. My friend Danny Wooder's mum used to buy them and we'd go through them like anything, guessing what kind of biscuit they were. Some were obvious but you got the odd tricky one! They all tasted great.

The crowds of shoppers attracted fly pitchers – un-authorised traders – who'd sell everything and anything: shitty watches, jewellery, perfumes, clothes, dodgy knocked-off gear that had been rejected in the factory. Danny's mum bought a shirt once for Danny's dad. She thought she was getting a really good bargain and it certainly looked alright in the packet. When she got it home the sleeves only came to half way between his elbows and his wrists. We were in stitches. So was the shirt, in all the wrong places.

One of the stalls sold empty paper carrier bags for five pence. They were ahead of their time! The environment might've been in a better state now if everyone had been doing things like that sooner.

The market offered endless entertainment to us kids. There was an organ grinder with a monkey that would hold out his tiny hat for people to drop their coins in. I loved that when I was little. We'd nick chestnuts from the chestnut seller when he wasn't looking, even though half the time they were too hot to touch, so we'd drop them on the ground. And we'd look out for a Sikh guy with a big colourful turban who'd wander down the street shouting, 'I've got a horse, I've got a horse!' His intention was to get adults to place a bet but instead he got a group of children following him like he was the Pied Piper, also shouting, 'I've got a horse, I've got a horse!'

When the BBC launched a new comedy series *Only Fools and Horses* in 1981 about a family of market traders, the Trotters, operating in Peckham, south London, the images they used for the opening credits were scenes from Chapel Market. I think the producers must have chosen that location even though it was the other side of the river from where Del Boy and Rodney lived because it perfectly summed up what a proper old-school working-class market was about. The first thing you saw when the credits rolled was the view over Chap from the Upper Street side, looking towards the Barnsbury council estate, and rows of market stalls mobbed with punters. To the right was the old Woolworths, and the Wimpy. Beyond that was the opening to our old estate, Mandeville Houses. To the left you could make out M. Manze's pie and mash shop as well as the flats at the edge of Barnsbury. My old primary school was off to the left and the flat my nan and grampa had on the estate, in Richmond House, was a bit further down. I was nine when the show started and I loved it. You can imagine the thrill of watching the biggest comedy show on telly and seeing all the places that were right on my doorstep. *Only Fools* ran for more than two decades and they never changed the opening.

In contrast to the buzz of Chapel Market was the Packington Estate, to the east of Upper Street. It wasn't high rise – more like loads of linked low-rise blocks, built in the sixties on Second World War bombsites. The blocks were connected by concrete walkways, which is a great idea if there's no real trouble but no one would ever say that about Packington. The police absolutely hated it because if you got away from them into the estate – which was a huge sprawl – they would never find you. I remember we used to play a game called 'Had' in the walkways. You could jump from one to another and no one would know where you were. It was impossible for people to catch you in those estates.

Packington Estate seemed to be the place where problem tenants were sent if they complained too much about their Asian, Black or Irish neighbours, so we were told. There were some pretty terrifying teenage gangs there. Some had mopeds and rode them on the walkways.

The proper gangsters were the next step up. You didn't mess with them. People would sometimes claim they were related to one of the main families if they got into a bad fight and were trying to stop getting their head kicked in. Kids usually knew who was connected and who wasn't, so if you had to say, 'My dad's with the so-and-so family,' the chances were he wasn't but it might just buy you a bit of time. Your attackers knew revenge would be coming their way if they made a mistake.

3

On the Rob

MY BROTHERS GOT ME INVOLVED IN BURGLARIES WHEN I was barely out of nappies. I was four years old I think, the very first time, maybe five. I would climb up roofs to get into shops through their skylights and then open the doors. A surprising number of places didn't have proper alarms back then. The skylights were so small that as Darren and then Scott grew bigger, I was the only one who could fit. A bit like Oliver Twist when Bill Sykes took him out to burgle and made him climb through a window. My brothers used to take me out robbing all the time but I wasn't aware that's what I was doing. I was too young. I just thought it was fun. They called me Spiderman because I was so good at climbing fences and walls.

I was the youngest person in my school with a digital watch. My brothers broke into Tesco looking for skateboards, which were the thing in the 1970s, and when they saw a big display of digital watches – which were a big thing too – they smashed through the counter and started filling their pockets, even clipping them round their necks. They got in by pulling back the metal shutters just enough to create a small gap. Darren was so skinny that Mark got him through it by greasing him up with Vaseline. Getting his head through was the trickiest part. Then he managed to open the big windows from the inside and let the whole of the estate in. Mums, dads, kids, the lot, cleaning out the whole store. They even nicked the tills.

When I was really small, I desperately wanted a bike, a little push bike with stabilizers, so Mark took me into Woolworths and said, 'Yeah, you choose any one that you want and I'll get it for you.' Ten minutes later I'd found the perfect bike. Mark came over and told me to ride it out the shop. Back then, they didn't put the pedals in; you had to screw them in later. So I was trying to cycle this bike with no pedals out of Woolworths thinking that he's actually bought something for me. Until I got stopped by the store security. Mark had a way of blagging everything and was all innocence, saying to me, 'Oh no, what are you doing, bro? You can't ride that. It's not ours.' They believed that a five- or six-year-old kid didn't have a clue, though by that point I kind of did. So I nearly had a bike, then I didn't.

I used to love going out with Mark when he was on the

rob. He was an expert at what we called the 'jump up'. Basically nicking shit off the back of a lorry. Mark would spot a van pulling up, then he'd either wait till the coast was clear and the back of the van was unlocked and quickly nick what he could before anyone noticed or he'd employ one of his scams. He had an instinct for what was the best approach and thieved so much he could recognize what sort of package was being delivered and to where. One scam involved walking right up to the driver pretending that he worked in the shop he was delivering to – 'All right, mate. You got a delivery for McColl's?' – and he'd sign the documentation and take the goods with no one the wiser. He was a great con artist, Mark. Very sharp and he could charm the birds from the trees when he put his mind to it.

If I was in the car with Mark I'd help him load it with whatever he'd nicked. Sometimes we'd be on foot, taking stuff from the back of vans then running it round the corner. Because we knew everyone in the market area we could run it into a shop or stall and it would be hidden. It was like that on the street, everyone looking out for each other.

Mark used to have one of those tiny little Fiats and then a proper old Mini. It was so small he could get away from the police by literally driving up on the pavements. He was a crazy driver but I loved it. I used to get such a thrill out of it. Sitting in the car with my brother Mark, I thought he was just the best driver in the world.

Another of his scams involved strolling into a newsagent or corner shop towards the end of the afternoon, then sneaking up the back and hiding in the attic or whatever. When the shop closed he helped himself to all the cigarettes. Cigarettes were good currency. There wasn't much in the way of security, so he could easily get out again. He'd sell them on to other corner shops further up the road and get 50 per cent of the value.

Christmas time was pretty mental, looking back. We all basically went out on the rob for the presents – it was almost like a competition to see who could come back with the best stuff. Christmas Day was spent comparing all the things we'd nicked for each other, sitting round the nicked Christmas tree, Mum popping in and out of the tiny kitchen, checking on the massive turkey she'd got from the market. Which she also nicked.

So going to school by day, then on the rob by night, or overhearing my brothers boasting about their escapades, was just my normal.

I was about six years old when I first saw the film *Bugsy Malone*. In hindsight, it's not an exaggeration to say that it changed my life. It was the first time I was aware that children could be in a proper film. I was completely transfixed. A whole film. All kids. About thieves and gangsters as well. A kind of old time, glamorized version of my real life, without all the shitty stuff!

I had my favourite TV shows of course. *Tiswas* was one of them. And everybody sat down to watch *Top of the Pops* on a Thursday night back then. Double act comedy shows were still the big thing. Mum loved them too so we'd all watch Little and Large, Cannon and Ball. Obviously Morecambe and Wise were amazing. The best of the lot, looking back. I was a huge fan of *The Two Ronnies*, though. My favourite bit of the show was the moment when Ronnie Corbett would sit in this huge chair and tell some rambling story, which always included the line 'the producer said'. I had no idea what a producer was and nearly all of it went over my head but I thought it was brilliant. Mum and my brothers would laugh so hard and that would set me off – you know how when you're a kid some things are so funny you almost can't breathe for laughing?

Mum used to love it when I did a little song and dance. We all liked Elvis and I'd do skits impersonating him, 'Suspicious Minds' or 'Jailhouse Rock', something to make her laugh. I remember feeling really special if I got time alone with her, being made a fuss of or even just being around her without my brothers – though I'd usually try to get her attention through some bit of showing off. One year, I was given a really cheap little organ player with a microphone and when Mum had friends round they would all egg me on to perform. They'd say, 'Come on, come on, get up. Here's ten pence if you do something.'

Ten pence seemed a lot of money then but I didn't need any encouragement. I was good at impersonating people, from my mum and her friends to the teachers at school and any sort of singer. I didn't think that I actually had that good a voice myself but I happily spent hours listening to singers and learning how to mimic them, note for note.

There was always music in the house, often coming from Mum's 'music centre', but even if she didn't put a record on there would usually be a radio playing somewhere. She was big on some of the crooners – Dean Martin, Perry Como, Matt Monroe, Nat King Cole, Bing Crosby and of course, Sinatra. Everyone loved Sinatra! My mum was really into soul and loved all the Motown and Stax stuff. Mum introduced me to so much great music. Reggae as well. Even though I was so young, I was soaking it all up. The old soul artists had such incredible voices and the rhythm and melody was so perfect. The lyrics so right. Everything just worked. My life-long love of black music culture came from my mum and I suppose hearing it still brings back memories and happy associations. I used to love hearing her sing along, usually when she was cooking or doing the dishes in her pinny. Her face would light up as the music took her away. It's funny how smells and sounds can draw memories up from some forgotten part of our mind. Sometimes I'll catch a sniff of a certain dish or hear a certain song and I'm back in my childhood. I can feel Mum's presence.

In the late 1970s, the band Madness were involved with a memorabilia shop about a minute's walk from my door. This was before they hit it big. I used to hang about there because even though I was only about seven I wanted to be a rudeboy. I was obsessed with the little badges everyone used to wear on their jackets. I used to go in there pretty much every day because it was so close. They were really patient with me. One day they told me they were going on tour. I wanted to go with them and eyed up this big trunk they had set out in the shop, thinking I could try to hide in it. It was amazing when they did become really successful. Bands like Madness and The Specials played music that was influenced by ska and reggae but with this punk energy. The Specials set up a label, Two Tone, that gave its name to this whole genre. They were anti-racist, it was all about white guys and black guys playing together.

My brothers were into that rudeboy culture in their DMs and Levi's, and with braces over their white T-shirts. Mark was a soul boy, listening to Alexander O'Neal and George Benson. They introduced me to Pink Floyd as well – they had a studio in Islington. Of course, nearly all the records we listened to were nicked.

I thought the world of my brothers and wanted to please them. It was a thrill and a kind of mark of respect when they made me feel involved. Of course, looking back, it was a crazy way to grow up but there was love. We all loved each other and we were a unit, a family, with my mum at the centre of it all and we all adored her. She was bold as brass, beautiful, fashionable, always ready with hugs and kisses and always ready to stick up for us.

In hindsight, I realize that she struggled much more than she ever let on to us. Even with all the petty thieving, we were pretty skint most of the time. There was no money coming from Mark's dad, whoever he was. Darren and Scott's dad was locked up, as was my dad by now. Mum smoked very heavily, as many did back in the day, and then the drink got hold of her – a social release that was part of the culture but for her it quietly became a secret addiction. We only found out years later just how much she was putting away every day. She was always slim but at best she had a terrible diet, then she slowly began eating less and drinking more. For all that my dad was a shit and she was better off without him, being left alone with four hyperactive boys was tough and lonely for her. She was sharp as a tack but had no money, no qualifications, education or formal training in anything. She did have a lot of informal training in stuff you couldn't exactly explain down the job centre. We always felt her deep affection for us and saw her strengths rather than her weaknesses. Somehow, through all that chaos, me and my brothers were happy, loved and looked after.

Mum worked part-time as a barmaid in the Spanish Patriots (which everyone called 'the Spanish Pats') on the corner of White Conduit Street. We used to go and sit in the back of the pub when she was working, and even as a young child I could see how everyone was drawn to her, that there was a warmth about her. She was a really sociable, likeable woman. She had a lot of hard knocks but she was always the life and soul of the party. Good energy. Good heart.

The pub was popular with local traders and our neighbours. They were a good crowd, generous too, and they really helped us out when the council decided to knock down Mandeville Houses and put us in a flat on Stonefield Street. The move was a big change for us. Our new home was part of an imposing Georgian townhouse, the kind of

Islington property that's very much sought-after now and worth a small fortune. In our day, the houses were a bit rundown, the street shabby in places, although already there were some well-off people in the area and houses were being done up. Ours had been too and the council had done a good job. Pretty much everything had been ripped out, the walls painted white, a new bathroom put in and a kitchen in a shade of orange that was so bright you needed sunglasses to look at it. It was a real step up from the old place, almost a mansion compared with what we'd had before. We had the ground floor and basement. When you opened the door to our flat you stepped onto a small landing with a narrow flight of stairs leading down to the bedrooms, with a door to the kitchen at the back and one to the living room at the front. The ground floor was all one big room but with a divider in the middle so you could make the place cosy. Just as well, as the living room had a high ceiling and big old-fashioned windows that were draughty. The way to get round that was heavy curtains, the heavier the better. Good quality drapes were a bit of a status symbol and ours were definitely the best, thanks to the Spanish Patriots and a pair of Arsenal legends.

The Spanish Pats was owned by Arsenal midfielder Eddie Kelly. Fellow player Frank McLintock had a pub called the Sutton Arms. Footballers weren't paid anything like they are now and often had a business that would bring in an income once their playing days were behind them. Eddie and Frank's businesses were connected in some way, I think. Mum knew both of them from working at the pub and got along with them well. By the time we moved she was ill, not that we had any idea how bad she was. Bad enough not to be working at any rate, which meant she was skint. When word got round, another friend and local businessman, Harry Hicks, got together with Eddie and Frank to organize a benefit for her to raise some cash. Tickets were sold and there were raffles and auctions arranged with some really good prizes. On the night itself, star players from Arsenal came to hand them out. The place was mobbed and the money raised was a pretty good indication of the love and respect people had for Mum. She was able to kit out the whole flat, which was lucky as we hadn't brought much with us from the old place. We hadn't much to bring. As finances had slumped, anything of any value had been pawned. Fair to say, there had been a few slumps.

Mum got us heavy green velour curtains with box pelmets and fancy nets. We had two velour sofas, also green, edged with a furry trim and tassels. The centrepiece in the living room was a large ornate fireplace in white stucco with gold trim. Above the mantelpiece was an enormous mirror with a reproduction gold frame. We'd swapped an olde worlde log cabin look for full-on opulence à la Palace of Versailles. At the centre of the new fireplace was our old much-loved three-bar electric fire. We had an antique style Chinese rug over a wall-to-wall golden-brown carpet. I remember when we got the carpet, the smell was amazing. I lay on it and closed my eyes, breathing in the scent of sheer luxury. We also had a new telly and hi-fi.

In the basement was Mum's room and a tiny room for Mark at the back that led out onto the garden we shared with the people upstairs. The bigger bedroom at the front was where me, Darren and Scott slept in a row of single beds. Our window was below street level and overlooked the bins. It could be whiffy in the summer with the window open, although probably no worse than the smells coming from three boys' worth of farting, smelly socks and all the crap we had lying about. In pride of place on our wall was a framed picture of Frank McLintock, a massive hero of ours. Frank had grown up in the Gorbals in Glasgow and moved to London when he signed for Arsenal where he went on the captain the team and lead us to our first ever European trophy as well as the League and FA Cup double. He was already a footballing hero and now a personal hero too. Even though I was just a kid, the move to Stonefield Street felt exciting. Like we were on the up. The good feeling turned out to be short-lived, though, because a year later everything changed again.

4

Saying Goodbye

I WAS SEVEN YEARS OLD WHEN I FIRST KNEW MUM was dying. The adults had been trying to hide the truth from us for a while but I had that sick feeling that something was badly wrong. I started spending more and more time with my friends Danny and Joanne and their family, the Wooders. It was almost like an open door for me at their house. I think Maureen knew that I wasn't happy at times but she didn't dig into anything. She probably felt I would open up if and when I wanted to.

I remember one day I was messing around in our bedroom with my brothers when Pat, a very good friend of Mum's, came in and said, 'Come here,' and I knew straight away. She sat us down and just said, 'Look, your Mum is very ill.'

Mum had cervical cancer. She was never one for going to the doctor. I don't know how long she had been poorly or whether anything could have been done if she had been diagnosed earlier, but I think by the time they found out what was wrong with her she was in a bad state.

I vividly remember seeing Mum in bed when we'd just been told that she was going to die and suddenly realizing how ill she looked. Before that moment, I'd always hoped she would get better. I got very upset at first. Very, very upset. They say I was completely inconsolable for a while and I cried myself to sleep every night. She was then taken to the hospital, St Barts down in Smithfield. It wasn't too long after that we visited her there for the last time, like a goodbye. I'll never forget seeing her sort of sat up in the hospital bed and looking basically yellow. She'd had chemo and everything but it hadn't worked. The room smelled awful. Like death.

I remember we went downstairs and saw a fountain with money in it and we got in and starting to take out all the coins. I'd never seen money in a fountain before. We were nicking all the money when Pat came out and slapped us around the head and made us put it all back.

Mum died in November 1979, a couple of months before my eighth birthday. She was only thirty-five. I'd been staying with the Freeds, who were then living in Rotherfield Street, but someone rang and I was walked over to our flat in Stonefield Street. I remember the grown-ups all sitting around a table and my mum's younger sister, Aunt Carol, saying, 'Your mum's died.' I was sort of expecting that day to come because we'd already said goodbye. I didn't cry. I just felt cold, numb and very alone. It was just me and my brothers now. No mum. No proper dad. I was so numb that I thought I had somehow come to terms with it. It took me many years to discover that this was far from the case.

Only Mark was allowed to go to the funeral, as the extended family thought me, Darren and Scott were too young. Instead we were sent to an auntie's place on their dad's side. It was actually only about twenty miles away but it could have been Wales for all I knew. I felt like a long journey and far away.

People have always told us it was one of the biggest funerals our estate had seen for years. It was amazing, literally amazing. We should all have gone to the funeral. We should have been able to say a proper goodbye to Mummy. On the day it took place, me, Scott and Darren decided to escape from the house and we just fucked off. We ran away. Obviously, they found us later but it was a weird feeling, knowing your own mum was being buried and just running and running through this strange landscape. We had no idea where we were going. We were trying to run off the pain and confusion of it all. Messed up, as any kids would be in that situation.

I suppose there had come a point where they knew Mum didn't have much time left, so the family got together to decide what to do with us. Mark was seventeen, so old enough to find his own place but not old enough to take over the tenancy of our council flat. Or 'the rent book' as people said. He found his own place to live – he was a pretty successful thief and had cash. Mum's half-sisters had their hands full with their own kids so it probably seemed like the best solution was for Carol to take over tenancy of the flat and officially foster me, Scott and Darren. But understandably, looking after three boys was too much and it wasn't long before Darren went off and lived with his Aunt Grace above a pub. The authorities would probably have been involved at some point as well, working out what was feasible. I think it was all planned with the best intentions. So in the end we were all split up and it was just Scott and me. It was horrible, being removed from two of my brothers when it felt like my brothers were all I had left.

Carol and her partner Mick seemed to take to Scott but not to me. Now, when I look back on it, I can see she probably tried to take to me, so I wasn't totally rejected, but I certainly felt unloved. I wasn't easy and the more I sensed that they didn't really like me, the worse I behaved. I was very messed up. I craved love and security but I didn't feel any. Once you lose your parents, or you've got no parents, you tend to think that no one can tell you what to do. I've always had a strong individualistic streak anyway, so anyone who tries to tell me what to do doesn't have it easy unless I've built up a lot of trust and respect. My aunt's boyfriend took it upon himself to be strict but I didn't feel he had the right to be. Mick was strict in a horrible loveless way. Cold and distant, sending a clear message: 'I don't want you here', 'Just do as you're told, keep quiet . . .', 'I'll put up with you because I have to'.

Mum had really hit it off with Maureen Wooder when I'd started going round their house and they had become good friends. Years later, Maureen told me that before she died, Mum had asked her to 'look after my baby', so that's why the Wooder family took me under their wing. I don't think Mum knew how much that would mean to me. Danny and his family are very close friends to this day and we still have holidays together, though now I can look after them.

Being over at the Wooders' was my great escape and I'd grab a few days there whenever I could. They had a big family of their own – Danny, his mum and dad, and then his four sisters, Jackie, Pauline, Debbie and Joanne – so it was a full house and they were bit stretched but they did the best they could, under the circumstances. I'd usually find a spot in Danny's room. They put up with a lot.

Joanne was a tomboy so she did the same things that me and Danny did and loved it. She didn't fight or steal though. We got up to all sorts. One day there was a heavy snowfall. We left the Wooders' house to go to school and made a little snowball and rolled it up the hill, rolled it and rolled it all the way to school. By the time we got there it was massive. And then after school, we rolled it all the way back down, going this way and that way to get the snowball going. It was the biggest snowball ever. Bigger than us!

When I stayed at the Wooders', their dad would always be up first and would make us a cup of tea and toast, then we got ready and were slung out the door to walk to school. Opposite their house was a park, like a field. Everyone called it 'the Temporary'. At Matilda Street, you crossed over the road and then you'd be into Barnsbury Park. We'd go through this little mini park, cross Hemingford Road and go through Barnard Park, which had a paddling pool in it and an adventure playground, which is where we used to hang out. It was a ten-minute walk but it could take twenty minutes. There was a bit with bollards and on the way back down the hill from school we'd get enough speed up to leapfrog over them.

Obviously we'd stop in the sweet shop to see what we could nick. Only Danny and I did that. Joanne was a good girl so if we went in the sweet shop she'd actually buy something. We felt like if she bought something we had the right to take something. It was buy one get one free – old-school style.

If we didn't go through the parks, the walk to school from their house was basically just one road but it used to feel like it went on forever. A neighbouring family had this old English sheepdog which used to meet us on the way and jump all over us. The Wooders had a beautiful red setter called Gentleman Sam. It's not like now where everyone's got dogs on leads. Back in the day, you just opened the door and the dogs were out like cats, roaming the streets.

Copenhagen Street, south of Matilda Street where the Wooders lived, was a bit tasty for outsiders back then but as we'd grown up there everyone knew us so we could walk the streets. There was a public toilet at the top of Richmond Avenue, where the Old Bill found a decapitated head. Darren, Scott and Mark used to scare us and say the guy that did it was still out there and hadn't been caught. So we used to do a proper sprint along that bit of the road past the toilets. I think it was a gangland thing but we never knew that because we were kids. Darren used to scare us to the point where Danny would run away, crying his eyes out. In fact, one night, he was so scared, a cab driver pulled over and said 'Are you alright mate?' and Danny got in his car. A stranger's car. Thankfully the guy was a proper taxi driver though and he took him home.

Before Mum died and we were all split up, the fighting at my house was pretty full-on. But that's just the way my older brothers were; they would all fight each other, then they would beat me up. I knew my brothers loved me but if there was a fight, as the youngest, I always came off worst. One of the great things about being with the Wooders was that at their house I wasn't at the bottom of the bullying chain. The environment in my house compared to the environment in the Wooders' house was such a crazy contrast because Danny had these nice big sisters looking after him. He liked having me like a brother though, even if I beat him at fighting. I had to have one brother I could beat.

Danny's dad used to have a great big old van. It was one of the old-fashioned furniture vans and we were obsessed with the idea of driving it. One day a neighbour ran up to Maureen's door and said, 'Your van's going down the road but I can't see anyone driving it.' Maureen ran out of the house and it was Danny and me – we were only very young but we'd taken the van! We managed to start it, having watched Danny's dad, then somehow got it into first gear before realizing that we were too short to actually see out of the window properly, or stop it. I think we took the keys from indoors. Some of the neighbours had a right go and started shouting. Maureen was more interested in getting us out. Thankfully the van got stuck on a kerb before we hit anything. We had a very lucky escape – that could have ended really badly. I still feel guilty about it!

While my mum was sick, Maureen knew I wasn't a happy little boy and I did start to talk about it a bit. But then after Mum died and I went from numb to inconsolable, it must have been obvious how lost I was. As the situation with Aunt Carol and her partner got worse, I virtually moved in with the Wooders for longer periods. Properly settled in. I wasn't aware then that Danny's mum had made that promise to my mum to look after me but I'll always be grateful that they were there for me and they welcomed me in.

I might have had no mum and no dad but, somehow, somebody cared.

5

Nothing Was Mine

MY GRANDPA, DONALD, WAS NEVER THE SAME AFTER Mum died. He was always kind to us but, even as a young child, you can tell when the light has just gone out from someone. He was a different person, though I only found out later how deeply depressed he'd become. Granny Florence had died a couple of years earlier and Mum had taken over cooking for him, as men of his generation just didn't really do that for themselves. After Mum had gone, he needed someone to make his meals so Carol used to cook for him and either me or Scott would run round the corner with it, on a hot plate, covered in tin foil, trying not to spill it. Quite tricky if there was gravy. Scott remembers one time he was playing football in the street with some cool guys he'd met, who were seriously good. Scott was pretty good himself, but he had to be at the top of his game to compete with them. Suddenly I cut right through the middle of them with a plate of food, daydreaming and singing to myself. The guys stopped and stared at me in disbelief, while Scott hoped I'd just keep going and wouldn't say anything, as them finding out I was his little brother would seriously cramp his style.

Even if I was off with the Wooders or the Freeds, I knew Grandpa's dinner time and so I'd often go to Stonefield Street to pick it up so I could deliver it. He'd give me a sweetie and I'd sit and chat away like kids do. Try to make him laugh. Sometimes we'd just watch the telly.

I didn't know how worried they all were about him. He tried to put on a brave face but my mum's early death just broke his heart. One really cold winter's night, in the early hours, not that long after Mum died, he walked out of his flat and down to the canal. He must just have picked a spot and laid down. He was found there the next day. They say he died of hypothermia. He just didn't want to go on without his Joanie.

When my mum died, I was pulled out of school. I remember going back, not wanting anyone to know what had happened, but they made an announcement in assembly. Kind of, 'Welcome back and we're sorry to hear . . .' Joanne thought it was such a bad thing to do. Some kids got awkward around me, trying a bit too hard to be nice. Others didn't even behave that well. I thought people were going to pick on me or bully me because kids can be horrible. And some did.

I was a seriously hyperactive child. I did everything. I was always busy, jumping from thing to thing. These days I would probably have been diagnosed with ADHD, post-traumatic stress, childhood abandonment issues, all that stuff, and they'd have maybe found a proper way of dealing with me and calmed me down. Instead, I was put into the special class at primary school for the naughty kids. Numerous times I'd be dragged down the stairs to her office by my headmistress Ms Thomas and I'd be punching or kicking her, acting like a lunatic. Poor woman. It can't have been easy for her. A school full of inner-city kids, with me as the cherry on the top.

I was constantly in trouble. I didn't give a fuck. I was wild, directionless and angry but underneath all the bravado was a scared, lonely and deeply insecure outsider, who craved affection, and acceptance. I found an excuse to fight with anyone I wasn't sure of, anyone who looked at me the wrong way. I suppose that was what my brothers had, quite literally, battered into me. If in doubt, fight.

Me and my brothers still basically lived on the streets. Everyone knew us. We grew up with some heavy London underworld around us and, because Mum had been well thought of and respected, there were always people looking out for us. People I didn't even know would come up to say they remembered Mum and tell me stories about her. They'd go, ''Ere you are,' and give me ten or even twenty quid. That was a lot of money back then.

We had free rein to do what we wanted. No one would touch us. Mark and the older kids hung about in the betting office and the younger ones, including me, would hang about the arcade, which was a few doors along. Some of the fly pitchers from outside the area would turn up with a suitcase to sell shitty watches, or something similar, either knocked off, faulty or both. Usually both. We knew they weren't welcome on our patch so if any of them gave us grief for hanging about, one of my brothers would go up to them, look them right in the eye, nick something from the case and run. The guy would chase after him, leaving the case behind. My job was to take the lot. The fly pitchers were dodgy but we were dodgier and if they'd tried to lay a finger on us, they'd get beaten up by proper local gangsters. They got to know us eventually and were on their guard. If they could, my brothers would sell on anything we managed to nick off them.

The Wooders would take me to their caravan in Clacton-on-Sea in Essex. Maureen knew we were all better off down in Clacton with sea air, beaches and proper wide-open spaces. A lot of mums felt the same. We called it 'the van'. In fact, we called the whole place 'the van'. 'We're going to the van.' It was just an ordinary caravan but somehow we all squeezed in. There was a whole network of Islington friends who had their own vans on their own little plots in Clacton. It was a real home from home.

We used to eat out quite a bit when we were at the van. We mainly went down the Sailor Boy during the day, a great big caff on the beach near Clacton's funfair. It had lots of traditional dishes: fish and chips, pie and chips, steak and chips – whatever you wanted, as long as you wanted something with chips. And we knew the people who worked there, a man called Terry and his wife Pat, who were lovely. I think Danny and I liked them so much we were actually remarkably well behaved. For us. We would more often cause 'murders' in Clacton though – 'murders' being a great old London expression for trouble.

We still had some discipline, especially from Danny's dad. He was very good with us but he had his rules. Especially about his car. We got seriously told off if we did anything wrong in the car. We weren't even allowed to eat sweets and absolutely no crisps or fizzy drinks.

The Wooders would also take us to the nearby Butlins, with Maureen getting us all nicely dressed and looking clean first. Back then, you could get a day pass and go in and have something to eat and drink. Us kids would go on all the funfair rides and, of course, the boats. Big mistake letting me and Danny anywhere near the boating lake.

'Biggest mistake I made in my life,' Maureen used to joke. 'They were tipping each other out of the boats. You name it, they were doing it.'

I think me and Danny are probably still barred from Butlins.

As well as visiting the Wooders, I used to go and stay with mum's sister Flossie sometimes on weekends and sometimes she'd look after me for longer periods. She lived with

Uncle Reggie and my two cousins, Debbie and Reg, on the Priory Green estate, which consisted of typical post-war council blocks. Her block had eight storeys with a courtyard down below, and backed onto the Caledonian Road, which we always called 'the Cally', near the Regent's Canal. It was pretty much next to the Barnsbury Estate and so close I could walk there, even when I was really little.

When she opened the door to me, she'd make me feel like this was the best thing that had happened to her all day. She'd give me a huge hug and always seemed to be laughing about something. It was a council flat, so nothing posh, but she'd done it up really nice. Very warm and welcoming. Just like my memories of her. She was a good cook too. She'd make her own pie and mash and a proper roast dinner on a Sunday. Everyone would be in the pub by twelve o'clock, but the joint would be in the oven. Her local was the Queens Head on the corner of Penton Street, where everybody knew everybody. Aunt Flossie had a seafood stall outside the pub on Fridays, Saturdays and Sundays. The family would muck in, joining her on the stall when needed, back in the pub when not. There was live music on a Sunday and anyone who could play and sing could grab a spot. One minute it would be a pensioner belting out an old music hall classic and then next the pub would erupt into Neil Diamond: 'Sweet Caroline, da da da'. You even used to get the pearly kings and queens down there. When the pub shut at 3 p.m., Flossie would put the tatties in the oven and put the veg on and do the gravy and lunch was ready.

Uncle Reggie was one of the nicest men you'd ever meet. He was a tradesman, but sometimes he used to take us down to Southend-on-Sea in his van. We loved Southend. It was probably already in decline as a holiday destination but still felt like a proper old-fashioned resort for Londoners. There was a pier and everything. The longest in the world. Fish and chips, ice cream and a huge fairground.

Flossie's sons from her previous relationship were a lot older than us. We only got to know one, Buster, who lived a few doors down with his wife Maggie. Maggie was really lovely and made a fuss of us if we went to see her, or she came over. Buster was alright with me and being younger I thought he was a proper tough guy. Darren used to say in reality Buster got beaten up more times than he can remember. Then he'd go around threatening to shoot everyone (he didn't really have a gun!) so Darren gave him the nickname Shotgun Buster, which was so funny it stuck for good. My main memory of Shotgun Buster is him sitting on the toilet, eating his breakfast, with the door open, so he could watch the telly. No shame about anyone seeing him. He literally sat there having a dump and eating a huge fry-up.

Although Aunt Flossie did make me feel loved and wanted when I was round at her place, still nothing felt permanent or really mine. The minute I was comfortable somewhere, it was time to leave, and I'd find myself back with Aunt Carol and her partner. It took a long time for me to realize that it's OK to love, accept and enjoy people on a deeper level. When I was a kid I learnt to mostly put the shutters up to protect myself from losing anyone else. Now, I love to be around warm and loving people and I know that you can feed off other people's energies and happiness. But back then I was just behaving in any way I could to find ways to escape the pain.

6

Anna Scher

I became obsessed with joining Anna Scher's drama group for kids in Islington, not far from our estate, after Danny and Joanne got in. The drama group had a policy that meant poor kids could enrol for 25p a week but there was a waiting list just to get an audition so they could see what you were about before taking you on. I got my name on the list right away. I was so desperate to join I'd go every week to find out if I'd reached the top. Anna knew Maureen Wooder and she kept saying to her, 'He keeps coming up, Maureen, he really, really wants to join, but I haven't got space yet.' But in the end, I drove Anna so mad that I got in. And I don't think I looked back from then on.

Anna was born in 1944, so she'd have been in her mid-thirties when I started but she always seemed ageless and sort of fascinating to me. She was originally from Ireland but her parents were Lithuanian and she's famously described herself as 'an Irish, Jewish, Lithuanian integrationist'. She originally started a performing arts school in 1968 in an Islington primary school. The demand was so high that the school moved to a converted mission hall on Barnsbury Road, which was renamed 'The Anna Scher Theatre' and established as a charity.

She was an inspirational teacher and really good at spotting and developing talent, but because so much of Islington was really rough back then, what she also wanted to do was to get kids like me off the street and help channel their energies. You knew she really wanted to help working-class kids, but she certainly didn't exclude middle-class kids. We all learned from each other, even though our home lives may have been very different. She wanted her kids to be as real as possible, wherever they were from. It's referred to as 'a natural delivery'. She taught us to improvise, having realized early on that a lot of the children turning up for her class weren't too hot at reading. Linda Robson went to Anna Scher's and put it well when she said, 'We weren't like drama school kids with jazz hands and tap shoes. Kids from Anna's did gritty drama like *Scum*.'

I discovered I genuinely loved acting, even the hard graft. We would learn monologues, plays, improvisation techniques – all that kind of stuff. Because I was so hyper and easily distracted, sometimes I must have driven the teachers round the bend. Luckily, they seemed to like something about me, enough to keep me on, anyway.

I was always trying to do stuff to entertain people, constantly craving love and attention. That whole perform-ance thing went hand in hand with a sadness that stemmed from how bad things were for me at home. Just like Danny's mum Maureen, Anna Scher could see my unhappiness. They both knew my history and understood how it affected me, long before I ever could.

Anna had a soft spot for me, probably because I'd made such a fuss about getting a place with her. And possibly because I stood out. In class, everyone would be doing as they were told and I would do something I was not meant to do. I stuck out like a sore thumb, really! Joanne says I was naughty but nice. A lovable rogue who came across as a happy-go-lucky kid, always with a massive smile. Big mouth, that's why! My party piece was putting my mouth round a full pint glass and swallowing half of it down.

I honestly believe that Anna Scher and the other drama schools that took in poorer kids were life savers. And not just in my case. There was a real mix of backgrounds in the classes and I learned a lot from that. I got to know kids I wouldn't have otherwise met. She really encouraged us to respect one another. The great thing about Anna and her team was that they used their skills to help a wide range of kids who needed support, not just the ones they thought could turn professional. Anna used to go to Belfast and do group work with kids from the two very divided communities there. She would get them improvising, so they would be talking. She was great at spotting talent but she wasn't just looking for that. She took every child seriously, whatever their ability, regardless of their prospects.

As I was starting out, there was a fashion for real working-class child actors in films and TV dramas, which meant there were many more opportunities for people like me to get roles. It was really good timing. One day, at the end of class, Anna took me to one side and said, 'Look, there are some people coming for an audition, can you make sure and be here next week?' The casting agents came along, watched the class and chose who they wanted. Luckily I was one of the ones to get picked. I even got three days off school – officially – and got paid. Happy days! I wasn't exactly going to win any attendance prizes anyway.

So I'd landed my very first professional role in *The Further Adventures of Oliver Twist*, a TV series starring Sir Harry Secombe. It was 1980 and I was eight years old. It was just a small part, basically hanging about looking all poor and shifty. Can't think why they thought I'd fit! They also made me understudy for the Artful Dodger, so I had to learn all the lines, which to everyone's surprise, I actually did.

Not long after *The Further Adventures of Oliver Twist*, I got my first tiny speaking part in the kids' TV series *Metal Mickey*. The show was about a normal family with a genius science boffin son who invents a robot called Metal Mickey to help around the house. The robot then becomes part of the family and all kinds of crazy adventures happen. The robot had a catchphrase, 'Boogie Boogie', that kids at school would copy. There were even a few hit singles 'sung' by Metal Mickey. Kids my age were fascinated by robots, outer space and anything remotely futuristic. And it was the era of *Star Wars* and R2-D2, a robot kids loved to impersonate. The show was a bit of a cult back then. It even came out as a boxed set not that long ago. Nostalgia for people around my age now!

The show was directed by Micky Dolenz of The Monkees and starred Irene Handl, who was an absolute legend. The Monkees were the first boy band, in a way, put together for a programme that aired on US TV in the sixties. They were mostly actors, including one English guy, Davy Jones. They had great songs, written by great songwriters and they were all good singers, so the music side of it was brilliant. People gave them a hard time because they weren't 'proper' musicians and had been put together but some of their stuff is considered classic now. Those Monkees episodes were brilliant. I was the second generation to see them, thanks to the BBC producer who had the bright idea to include them in UK kids TV programming, so a new generation was able to discover them.

Even though my part was small, not a main character or anything, it was great to feel like a little cog in something like that. Every young actor gets excited about their first speaking part on film or TV and back then it was even more important because you'd only get your full Equity card and be part of the union when you'd had speaking parts. I was still very young so it was even more exciting.

I seemed to get on well with Micky Dolenz, and I guess

he was impressed enough with my audition to cast me, which was a huge thrill because I loved the Monkees. We rehearsed down at Elephant and Castle, just south of the river, in what I think was a town hall or recreation centre. Irene Handl, who played Granny, was lovely. She was nearly eighty when filming for *Metal Mickey* started. She had done some extraordinary work, appearing in more than a hundred films, including classics like *I'm All Right Jack*, *Brief Encounter* and *The Italian Job*, with Michael Caine. She'd also been in a couple of early Carry On films, which were always being shown on telly back then. She was iconic. I was a huge fan and so was everyone I knew. My mum had always loved Irene Handl, too. All that meant it was really special for me to be working alongside her. Irene had a very distinctive voice – real old London. Cockney, but with her own twist. She was so funny. Her comic timing was impeccable – her body language, her expressions, the way she intonated everything she said. If there was any comedy to be got from a script, she'd find it and nail it, make it her own. She died in 1987, but any time her name comes up people still say, 'Oh, Irene Handl, she's a legend'. I was quite nervous about meeting her but she was very sweet and, to this day, I'm honoured to have worked with her, even for a short time. And glad I behaved myself, for once. I think I felt I'd be letting Mum down if I pissed off someone she had been such a fan of.

So there I was, a fan of *Metal Mickey*, Micky Dolenz *and* Irene Handl. You can imagine how nervous and excited I was to actually be working with them on one of my favourite programmes as well as one of the most popular kids' shows at the time. With me being so young, the adults looked out for me. I think they were aware that it was one of my first jobs and everyone was helpful.

I was playing a lost, runaway kid that the family found in their house. I was really determined to focus on my character and not mess up. Micky Dolenz was great; he made me feel relaxed and let me do my thing. The show was recorded in front of a live studio audience in the main ITV studios on the South Bank. The studio set was the interior of their 'house' and I remember they sat me down at the kitchen table and I did my whole little street urchin thing. It was fascinating to see how a popular show like that was made. To be inside looking out, when before I'd been glued to the show every week and seen the very same set, but as an actual house, was amazing. I had a totally different perspective. The lighting and studio equipment was huge. The cameras moved about on platforms with wheels, like giant dodgems. The studio audience was a good thing because you felt a buzz from them, which added to the whole experience.

A little while after *Metal Mickey*, Micky Dolenz crossed my path again. He was starring in a theatre production in London of my absolute favourite childhood film *Bugsy Malone* and the producers approached Anna Scher to say they were looking for kids to cast.

Micky obviously already knew me from before and as we'd got on well, I thought I was at least in with a good chance. I was so excited. To be in a *Bugsy Malone* musical was a dream for me.

Anna chose ten of us to go for the audition, which was in a big dance studio. When we got there the place was all full of kids from Sylvia Young, Barbara Speake, Italia Conti . . . Top posh drama schools where the kids were properly trained in singing and dancing. Anna's school wasn't really like the others. She specialized in film and TV roles and had a rule about not putting her kids up for parts in adverts. We did a bit of theatre stuff, but not much. I don't know if she had found out about the *Bugsy Malone* audition late on, or if it just wasn't her thing, but for some reason what we'd prepared for the audition was a bit cobbled together at the last minute.

We did our usual warm up. Silly things like 'Head, Shoulders, Knees and Toes'. Then 'Betty Butter' type tongue twisters. 'Red Lorry Yellow Lorry', 'Peter Piper picked a peck of pickled pepper'. Our audition piece was the Beatles song, 'Yellow Submarine'. We'd only had a few goes at that, so were still a bit ropey.

I watched in a kind of jealous horror as all the kids from the posh drama schools, who totally had their shit together, did proper full-on song and dance routines from famous musicals. Then we went in, kind of waved our arms about a bit and sang 'We All Live in a Yellow Bloody Submarine'. None of us got the job. So that was that. I do love the Beatles. Pure genius, even 'Yellow Submarine'. But I still cringe when I hear the song and remember that terrible audition. I was gutted.

From early on, I knew I couldn't take anything for granted in acting. Nothing was in the bag. You always had to work hard and try your best. There were jobs I went for that I really wanted and didn't get. It definitely kept me on my toes.

I loved going to Anna's classes every week. Loved every minute of it and I never wanted them to end. It was important not to miss sessions and I was so careful not to be late. Although I was still naughty, by my usual standards I was a saint. We all so much wanted to get picked for stuff and knew we had to work hard to make an impression. The atmosphere was incredibly competitive but I thrived on it. It was like the opposite of kids waiting for the school bell to ring so they could go home. I didn't want to go home. I felt like I belonged in Anna Scher's drama group in a way that I didn't back at Stonefield Street.

7

The Wooders

I was living two different lives. When I was staying with my Aunt Carol and spending more time with my brothers, I was fighting and thieving. It was so different to being with the Wooders where I felt accepted and not just put up with. Don't get me wrong, the Wooders weren't a family of librarians. You had to be shrewd, well-connected and tough at times to keep afloat in business in that area at that time. But there was also loyalty and respect, and at home the family was loved and looked after. Looking back, I know it was an important thing for me at the time that the Wooder family had a mother figure who was kind and loving and funny and a father figure who was more strict but also fun, funny and generous – they were what I needed.

The Wooders gave me a taste of the proper loving family that I craved so much, treating me the same as their own kids. They had a spacious open-plan living room with a kitchen on one side and a dining bit in the middle. We always sat down at the table at tea time ('dinner time', if you're middle-class), seven or eight of us. It was good, simple comforting food like buttery jacket potatoes and Oxo or Bovril drinks. Everyone would be talking and laughing, there was a real family atmosphere. It felt normal – not that I knew what normal was. At those moments, I felt as if I was part of a real family where everyone got along. Maureen still says about Danny and me: 'They just acted as if they were two brothers and I never looked at it in any other way.'

When Maureen goes to see her granddaughter now, that's the only time they all sit round the table together because 'Nanny' is there. Maureen still insists on it. She's old-fashioned that way. I still feel, to this day, there's a real connection between food and togetherness. That feeling almost definitely stems from those evenings with the Wooders.

But despite the welcome I got from my surrogate family, I was still a deeply traumatized little kid. When I stayed over at the Wooders' house I slept in the back bedroom with Danny. I used to wet the bed and I didn't want to let anyone know. I'd be up all night trying to dry my sheets and my pants. Joanne remembers I used to be on the landing where the heater was, drying my wet things. She would think, 'Oh my God, he's wet the bed again.' It made her sad to think about it. I thought if I dried things out no one would know. Danny wasn't aware of what was going on, he was too young, but his older sisters and parents knew. No one said a word to Danny because they knew I felt ashamed.

The bed-wetting didn't stop for years.

And I wasn't just having problems when I stayed with the Wooders. Sometimes when I was with my Aunt Carol in Stonefield Street, I used to get so scared of going to the toilet, I'd stand and piss on the carpet. You know when you're little and you hear radiators creak at night or some strange sound in the house and you go, 'What's that noise, what's that noise?' Your imagination takes over. Little things used to totally freak me out. All this made me even less popular around the house, with more angry whacks from my Aunt Carol's partner, Mick, and general verbal abuse. I don't think they had any idea what was going on with me. I can understand now how frustrating this must have been for Carol. Not only was I a handful, but one who would wet the bed and piss on carpets. The more scared I was the more I would freak out at the slightest thing, so yelling at me made it likely to happen more often. I was terrified of the dark. Memories of my dad beating up mum up and then coming for us would come rushing back, as well as all the usual ghouls and monsters kids dream up at night. I used to hide any fear or upset and wouldn't talk to anyone about what was going on. I worried how people would react, that I'd be thought of as weak. I felt I could never show weakness, definitely not with my brothers.

I remember being at Barnsbury Park and Darren being so angry with me about something that he started chasing me around a car. Joanne was there and she ran with me. We were running round and round trying to get away, though there was no reason for her to run, as Darren wouldn't lay a finger on a girl. He got so frustrated he just jumped over the car and Joanne was pleading with him not to hurt me, shouting, 'Don't, don't please stop it!' None of us remember what it was about.

Don't get me wrong. There was no premeditated violence from Darren against me. He loved me, there was never any doubt about it. Darren would have fought to the death for his family but when he lost it, even with us, he really lost it. He was terrifying, powerfully built, strong for his age, utterly fearless, with a real talent (if that's the right word) for fighting. He seemed almost possessed by some inner demon when the red mist came down. Sometimes I'd hide at Danny's house.

To be fair to Darren and Scott, it wasn't just me left without parents; we were *all* alone and totally damaged. I was naughty, a cheeky kid, and sometimes my brothers used to try to put me in order. I acted like I didn't have a care in the world and they took it on themselves to look out for me. Darren was always tough, he'd learned he had to be, but he also had my back. He was also a victim of some extreme stuff growing up. Because Darren was four years older, he got even more shit from my dad than I did and, as a consequence, was full of rage. He was only twelve when Mum died, a terrible age to lose her. He wanted to toughen me up the only way he knew how. I was always small for my age, and he was obsessed with me being tough enough to be able to stick up for myself. Though, thinking about it, I may not have had to stick up for myself quite so much if he hadn't kept getting me into extra fights. We were a very boisterous family, anyway.

My friend Danny kind of liked being around it, funnily enough, coming from a family of girls. We used to box each other. His mum and dad gave us some money to go out and buy a nice outfit, I think it was for Christmas or a party or something, but we came back with boxing gloves and proper shorts like boxers wore, and started punching the life out of each other. Their kitchen was big and that became our boxing ring. We used to square up to each other and box until we fell over – or were crying. Whichever came first. Just as well we were both only little and couldn't do much harm. Joanne says it was generally me beating Danny. Well, I was older, wasn't I?

Thinking back, there was probably a bit of bullying there on some level. I was getting beat up by my brothers so maybe I thought I'd beat Danny up. I was like, 'Put the gloves on Danny, let's go a few rounds.' I would be getting the better of him so he would take the gloves off and grab me by the ears. That wasn't in the Queensberry

Rules! Little did I know that Danny would grow up to be a lot bigger than me. Just as well he's got no desire to box me now.

For a time, Penton Primary had me, Darren and Scott to contend with. Darren was the fighter in his year, Scott was the fighter in his year and I was made to feel I should be the fighter in mine. Darren used to start trouble and I would have to join in and fight his battles. He was my brother after all. It was expected.

We were always in some kind of trouble. Not necessarily fighting every time, just getting up to mischief. It was fun as well. We used to go down Chapel Market 'at dinners', which was what we called our school lunch break. We went off to Tesco to steal family packs of Mars bars, Milky Ways, all sorts, then took them back to sell at school in the afternoon. We set up a little tuck shop and with the proceeds of our ill-gotten gains, we'd play a game called 'up the wall', which I got totally obsessed with because of the great gambling potential. The stakes would be a penny up the wall or 10p, 50p, whatever we had. It was straight-forward really. You'd throw stuff at a wall and see who could land theirs nearest to it. They would win. You could throw anything, from cards to marbles to coins, as long as whoever was playing was throwing the same kind of stuff. Coins were best as I'd get to keep them if I won, though I often lost all the money I'd made from the nicked sweets tuck shop.

A lot of the playground entertainment was based

around games that went back generations. Anything with gambling potential appealed to me, including marbles. Everyone seemed to have marbles. I don't know why, they just did. There were two games of marbles – the fun type with no risk involved and the serious competitive game, when your whole marble collection was up for grabs. No prizes for guessing that I was obsessed with the risky version.

Our version was a simple hit and take kind. The first person rolled their marble then the second rolled theirs and aimed to hit it. Alternate turns were taken by each player until one hit the others. That marble then became their property. This could sometimes take ages and it could stretch right around the block if the marbles rolled into the gutter.

If I lost at the gambling games there were others that were basically an excuse for a fight. British Bulldog was the perfect game to take down your enemy. The game started with one 'Bulldog' that faced up to a number of kids. The Bulldog would run around the playground and any kid they captured become a fellow bulldog. Eventually, there would be as many bulldogs as there were runners and carnage would ensue as personal vendettas were acted out in the name of 'playing'. Any underhand tactics came into play to dish out punishment. Unsurprisingly, the game is banned by many schools nowadays. I used to love it.

We also had another version, where once you were caught, you joined arms with your captor. This would eventually lead to a long line of people to penetrate if you were looking to stay in the game. It also led to many people being clothes-lined by the eager line of bulldogs.

I had a totally addictive personality so it's not surprising that, along with the thieving, I got hooked on gambling when I was still in primary school. We also used to smoke. Darren got me started at the age of four. There was a sweet shop called Frankie Stones where you could buy 'singles' – single cigarettes. At primary school, we would nip out for a cigarette. Even Joanne had been a smoker, though she gave up at the ripe old age of eight.

I also experimented with alcohol from a young age. As you came down the stairs in the Wooders' house in Matilda Street there was a little black cupboard where the booze was kept. Among other things, Danny's dad used to run nightclubs and pubs, so that was probably where he got some of the booze we helped ourselves to. The minute their mum and dad went out Joanne, me, Danny, and probably Joanne's friend Ashley, and whoever else was about, used to raid the cupboard and make cocktails, even though Joanne and me were only about twelve and Danny was ten. We mixed all kinds of drinks and tried them. We'd make up names for our disgusting cocktails thinking ourselves very grown-up. I remember making 'snowballs', although what went into them I couldn't tell you. We only took a tiny bit out of each bottle then topped them up with water. We'd go for the mad-looking bottles that family friends had brought back from holidays because no one was going to drink them anyway. Weird green concoctions at the back of the cupboard nobody else ever touched. If they'd ever checked on them they must have thought the colour was fading, the green getting lighter and lighter and lighter.

We'd smoke too. If we heard Danny's dad pull up in the car we'd go, 'Oh my god, he's back!' and put the cigarettes out on the wall in the hallway. Danny's dad didn't smoke but he must have been able to smell it. And even if he couldn't smell the cigarettes, he wouldn't be able to miss the embossed wallpaper smouldering away where we'd stubbed them out. We didn't think of smoking as being bad for us back then; it seemed glamorous. Crazy really.

The school bully at Penton was a lad in the year above us. One time, I ended up having a fight with him, the two of us scrapping all the way down the stairwell, slugging it out on the concrete stairs.

I was good friends with Peter Gordon, who was in the same year as me and Joanne. She was friends with him too. He was fun, naughty, another lovable rogue. It was why the two of us got along so well. Peter was boisterous and he could stand up for himself. He wasn't the type to take shit from anyone. We used to go fishing down the canal and Joanne and her friend Ashley would turn up. There was a phase just starting at school where we all thought we should have boyfriends and girlfriends, even though we had no idea what that meant. Peter and Ashley decided to pair up and even though Joanne was like my family we decided to be boyfriend and girlfriend. It all came to an abrupt halt when Peter got a huge pot of maggots from somewhere and I thought it would be funny to throw them over the girls.

They screamed and cried. Joanne ran all the way home in a right state, shaking herself, trying to get the maggots off. She was distraught. I was living with the Wooders at this time and when I got back Joanne's mum gave me a clip round the head.

I think part of the reason I was naughty was because I felt I didn't have anyone to tell me what to do. I was never worried about going home and getting a row because once Mum died, who could tell me off? I felt like Aunt Carol and Mick didn't much care what happened to me outside when I was out of their sight. I'd only be likely to get a backhander off Mick if I misbehaved. We got into a routine of basically ignoring each other. I was pretty much living with the Wooders quite a lot of the time anyway, which probably suited Carol and Mick.

Maureen Wooder had a way with kids. I loved her so much and although I was obviously naughty, she knew instinctively how to deal with it. She wouldn't take any shit but she somehow handled nearly everything with humour. I wanted to please her, so I made sure to balance out the stuff likely to put her back up with being loving and nice. She showed me a lot of love which meant so much to me that I didn't want to step out of line. I sensed how far I could push things. I would have been devastated to lose her love and affection. Aunt Carol knew I was safe and happy there. Maureen kept her informed so she knew where I was and what I was doing. Even though I wasn't happy at home, Carol was my legal guardian and Maureen respected that. The two of them were on good terms.

8

To the Van

THE BAD ATMOSPHERE IN THE FLAT WITH MY AUNT Carol and Mick affected how I got on with Scott. We were usually scrapping. Sometimes for fun, sometimes not. I can understand why even Scott was sometimes relieved when I was away at the Wooders. Things would have been a lot quieter.

I loved Scott, he was my brother, but I couldn't help feeling sad and jealous that he seemed to fit in at home. They seemed to like him. I suppose the more I sensed that they didn't like me, the harder I made it for them to warm to me. I closed down any emotion and stayed away as much as I could, only going back when I had to.

It wasn't terrible all the time, though I had days of being almost impossible to deal with. We had moments when

74

things felt better at home, happier for me, and at those times I was easier for Carol to handle and the atmosphere was a lot nicer. One treat I did look forward to with Aunt Carol and Mick was when we sometimes went for posh fish and chips on a Friday. There was a famous fish and chip shop with a restaurant in Lisson Grove, a few miles south-west, that we liked. It was special, the atmosphere buzzing and friendly and the food was great. Moist fish inside crunchy batter and chips made with good potatoes and perfectly fried. Big portions. Fish and chips can be so good when they're done well. I have good memories of those occasions.

I always loved my food and was excited by any new flavours but I don't remember ever being taken to an Indian or Chinese restaurant, even though there were loads around. It was always traditional places for fish and chips or pie and mash. At home, we sometimes had a proper traditional roast on Sunday, with all the trimmings. That always felt like a treat.

Any kind of break from school, half term, bank holidays, saw the Wooders back at 'the van' in Clacton again. They knew I was desperate to go with them so most of the time they took me along – any time there was a chance to go to the van I'd jump at it. These were real happy times. Clacton was a physical escape from my troubles, though of course, wherever I went, trouble soon followed.

However long we spent there, the routine was pretty much the same. Danny's dad would put us in the back of a van and halfway there we'd all be thinking, 'Are we nearly there yet?' London is so huge it seemed to take forever to get any distance. There was a big block of flats over by Hainault, in the part of Essex that's on the edge of London. Those flats still haunt me. Whenever I see them they remind me of looking out of the of the van window and thinking, 'Shit, we're still only halfway to Clacton. We've got ages to go.' Danny and his sisters feel exactly the same. I know everything feels like it takes ages when you're a kid but it feels even longer when you're being slung all over the place in the back of a van with maybe a mattress to sit on and all the stuff you're taking to the caravan around you.

On one holiday when Danny was about eight or nine his dad got him his first bike, a little 80cc trials bike. We were so excited about it, the way kids are about any kind of vehicle, and we'd be out at the crack of dawn, outside the van, starting up the bike, revving it, making a terrible racket. We always stuck together. If we were pissed off we took it out on the bike. If I kicked the bike, Danny would kick the bike. He was that bit younger and would copy me.

Maureen said we never took any notice of anyone. She had loads of rows with us, going mad for waking everyone up, so we used to go down to the empty beach and ride all the way round it on the bike. Back and forward, over and over again, while everyone else was still in bed in their vans. It was brilliant fun. We were the coolest kids, thanks to that bike. In the end, the site put a stop to people having motorbikes, probably because of us.

Maureen used to call us 'the terrible twins' or 'the terrible twosome'. She was out for a walk one day and heard a right old din. When she went to see what was going on, there was Danny and me punching the life out of a boy. I think Danny might have started that one, then I stuck up for him.

The kid we were fighting was about six foot seven, and there was Danny and me about three foot two! The lad was from Brixton, in south London. Brixton had a name for being notorious and rough and we were a little bit worried when we ran into him. I said, 'No, no, no mate, we don't want no trouble, no trouble whatsoever.' It was a bit of a stand-off. Then Danny jumped up and head-butted the guy. He fell back and I jumped on him. Maureen had to dive in and break it up. We got a right telling off.

Right after, we actually got to know the guy. Next thing we were best mates, even though we'd hated him to start with. Not only was he not on our patch of the caravan park, he was from south London! We called him Brixton Mickey.

At the caravan park there was a clubhouse with an arcade. We had a special one-armed bandit we always played. One of us would play then then the other would take over so no one else got a chance to get anywhere near this particular machine. That was because we'd found a way to fiddle it. We had a hooked wire, a bit like the kind you get on a strimmer, and we put it in the slot where the coin went, then we could click it back and get a credit. Click, click, click. Over and over. Brilliant, and we discovered it!

There were other machines as well, and some of them you could tip a bit. With those it was pretty straightforward. Give the machine a nudge and you'd get the odd coin. People thought we were in there losing money but we were actually hoarding our winnings. We'd come home with a bag of coins and stick it out of the way under the bed. It sometimes looked like a lot of cash but it was all pennies and two pence coins so not as much as you might think. Maureen obviously didn't know we were fiddling the machines and couldn't understand what we were up to down there.

At the caravan, we'd be out all day then get ready for the night, what we called the club hours. You know, shower, put your best clothes on, look the part. Get down to the clubhouse to play pool. Joanne remembers that it was a big thing for her to get all dressed up to go the clubhouse. She might just be meeting people she knew from home but it felt different, more exciting. Danny and I went too, every day when we weren't barred. There was no social media, no smart phones, so if you wanted to meet people and mix with them you would actually have to go out. For us, the clubhouse was the height of sophistication. Though it really wasn't posh at all. There was a shitty DJ, the odd band. It was like a large bingo hall, basically, with tables and everyone sitting round. We'd go in, claim our table for the night, then leave Maureen to hold the fort while everyone else took off and went to the bar, or played on the arcades or the pool table. We were more interested in running here, there and everywhere. The adults would be at the tables, with regular trips to the bar for the next round of drinks, which may have helped make the entertainment seem a bit more entertaining than it really was.

At the end of the night, Maureen would have to come out looking for us, especially Danny and me. We were never going to come home otherwise, were we? She was the kind of woman who would literally shout out the window, 'Danny, Sid, Joanne – HOME'. You could hear that from miles away . . .

I probably led Danny astray. We got a lot of freedom at Clacton because Danny's dad wasn't around all the time. He would drop us off and then go back to London because he had business to do. Maureen tended to be easy-going, maybe because she'd had four girls and thought she could leave me and Danny to get on with it. She probably thought 'boys will be boys' and that us getting into the odd scrape was part and parcel of life. It was all fun and having a bit of independence helped us grow up and learn from each other. And it was nice for Danny to have me wasn't it? Without my influence, he could have turned out a different person. And without his, I could have turned out even worse! The atmosphere around the Wooders was such a contrast with my life in Stonefield Street. There, I didn't feel as if I fitted in. With the Wooders I felt loved and appreciated. There were ground rules, restrictions on what we could do, and the structure was a good influence on me. The girls listened to their mum and dad, so me and Danny did too. I always deeply respected them, even when I was being naughty.

As Maureen says, 'We all just sort of worked in with each other.'

I loved being part of their big, happy family. Everyone got on. No one was better than anyone else, everyone was equal. It was great for me, being treated like a baby brother by Danny's sisters. We had good times with loads of laughter – enough to outweigh the trauma and trouble in my background. Or, at least, for a little bit. When you have a laugh somehow nothing else matters. It's just you and the people you're with, laughing and joking and bouncing off each other, getting vibes from each other. There ain't nothing like it. You can't buy that kind of happiness. It's universal, the best there is. I know people who've come from diverse backgrounds and experiences and that's all they want. It's all anybody wants. Unconditional laughter and love.

It was totally different from my own family. There was no real fighting in the Wooders' house. Last thing, when everyone was in bed, someone would call out, 'Goodnight, John Boy.' Then you'd hear, 'Goodnight, Danny.' 'Goodnight, Joanne.' 'Goodnight, Sid . . .' We were like the Waltons!

I thank the Wooders so much for what they did for me. I will never forget it. At the same time, I always knew that, however kind they were, the Wooders weren't really my family. I was a visitor and the time always came when I had leave and go back to my real life, to my foster parents. And to my brothers. I loved them but they were maybe even more messed up than I was.

9

Rich and Poor

WHEN I WAS GROWING UP IN ISLINGTON IT WAS A REAL mix – all kinds of housing, all kinds of people. Me and Danny sometimes used to walk up to Richmond Avenue, which was the posh street across from Barnard Park. Beautiful four-storey townhouses. Tony Blair lived there, long before he became prime minister. Eddy Grant, the singer, had a house there. We got to know him a bit. He'd chat away with us if we spotted him, which was a big thrill as we loved his music. I still do. Su Pollard from *Hi-De-Hi!* also lived in the nice bit of the neighbourhood. Off Richmond Avenue was a little crescent called Thornhill Square, where the actor Michael Crawford lived. Me and Danny knew who had money and who didn't because of the way their houses were done up and the cars they had.

David Rappaport from *Tiswas* had a smart MG Midget, I remember. We'd wash the rich people's cars to make a bit of money.

So at the top of Richmond Avenue were the people with money, and then at the bottom of the street were squatters who kept geese. I did say it was a real mix! All around was council housing, like my family's place in Stonefield Street. Then you got working-class grafters like the Wooders who took up the right to buy and were admired for having done well for themselves.

The squatters I remember were all musicians, jazz and prog rock, that kind of thing. Interesting people with beautiful though beaten-up old Citroen DS cars, like the cool ones in the Pink Panther films. The squats weren't at all squalid. The occupants were probably hippie types with wealthy parents, quite posh really. You could tell from the way they spoke and behaved. Me and Danny would wander in and out as boys. We'd be in the back gardens messing about. They wouldn't invite us in as such, but it was like an open house arrangement. They used to entertain us and we entertained them, so it was all good. We were intrigued by them as they were so different from us.

There was a communal area at the back of the Wooders' house in Matilda Street with stables which were used by a nice old guy called Ernie. He looked like someone from the country. Not only that, but someone from the country from another era, in his flat cap and tweeds, riding around on a horse and cart. He had a few horses and some donkeys. I think he even had some goats for a bit. There were chickens as well so at the Wooder's house we'd have a cockerel cock-a-doodle-dooing at fucking six in the morning. If there was an event going on, a school fete or something, he'd provide horse and pony rides. Every now and then there would be big hay bales dropped at the front of the houses and we'd play on them before he put them away.

Now when I tell people there were stables at the back of the houses they are like, 'Really?' They can't believe it; it's so near the centre of such a huge city. It seemed normal to us in Islington, in the 1970s and '80s. Some of the communal area was used to give people proper gardens, the rest given over for building mews houses and apartments.

Maureen always says, 'It was just like a worker's place, Islington. We were all the same really. There was nobody better than anyone else, I loved it, warts and all.'

Back then, there were lots of pubs. To get from Matilda Street to school you would have to go up Copenhagen Street, past the Nelson pub, and then another pub called the Mitre. I always remember the pub by Barnard Park. It became the Lark in the Park, but back then it was the George. There used to be a little bit in the George, like a tuck shop, where you could buy a bag of crisps and a bottle of fizzy drink or something. It wasn't in the main bar bit, there was a little separate section with its own door.

For all the changes in Islington over the years, there is still poverty. The old houses that survived demolition have become seriously posh and eye-wateringly expensive but the big estates are still there, so it's a complex set up. The bigger town houses where our local celebrities lived on Richmond Avenue started as a single property and were relatively cheap. Now they're nearly all split into flats and even they cost a fortune. Crazy. Millions for a house! A million for a flat! Stupid stuff. The only way you can afford to buy there now is if you make a ton of money – or inherit. Some of the most sought-after Georgian properties, the ones that have been done up, are right on the edge of the Barnsbury Estate. You get respectable middle-class professionals who send their kids to private school living alongside people struggling to feed their kids and pay the electricity bill. People without much, living cheek-by-jowl with houses that cost the earth. Displaced kids growing up surrounded by huge wealth. The contrast is stark. There is a massive divide between rich and poor, much bigger than even it was before when I was growing up and we had a few TV stars up the road and hippies in squats.

No one nicked from each other. Whether you were from a council house or were privately housed, everyone got together and was involved so it didn't feel as if there were any divisions. I mean, there was a rough element, like me and my brothers, but as rough as we were we knew who to respect and what was not OK. We were poor but would all look out for each other. We'd nick from shops, but there was an honour code when it came to our neighbours. Rich or poor. You wouldn't nick from your own and you wouldn't grass on anyone who may have been a bit naughty somewhere else.

Crime has changed as well. It's not just the old-school stuff – serious drugs have moved in, especially into the estates. If that had been going on when I was a kid, given my family's problems alongside my try-anything bravado and addictive personality, as well as other issues I'll come to later, I'd be dead now.

One of the biggest feelings of failure as a kid is if you feel excluded. Whatever background you're from, one of the most important things is to feel accepted. I knew all about that after my mum died and I have sympathy for other people who've also felt like that. A lot of the petty fighting and thieving I got involved in was about feeling included, part of something, I realize now. It wasn't that different to the performing I liked so much – the whole, 'Look at me, I can act, I can sing,' was about wanting to be loved. I can so easily understand how when kids aren't loved and the gangs come and say, 'You're one of us. Look at you, you can fight, you can thieve,' it's tempting. I might have had no mum, no dad, but somehow there were people in my life, families that cared enough. I know that lots of kids don't have even that and it makes absolute sense that they get led off down the wrong path, that they make mistakes early on that they can't come back from. I thank God I had the Wooders and that I could channel my energies into acting at Anna Scher's drama school. I think there's even less for poor kids growing up in similar areas now. There are fewer opportunities to find a way out and definitely less of a community feeling that even if your neighbourhood is rough you're part of something and there are people looking out for you.

In 1981, when I was nine, there was a huge community party for Lady Di and Prince Charles's wedding. There was a dump with corrugated iron fencing and a temporary playground coming up onto Barnsbury Park, and the children painted the fences red, blue and white. The only way to control kids was to give them something to do. So we were given a tin of paint – it didn't matter where it came from, as long as the fences were painted.

They shut the streets down for the Charles and Di wedding party. People got together and divvied up who was in charge of what. They called it 'the club'. Someone would go round and collect maybe £1 or £2 a week off each family, so at the end of it, they had quite a bit to buy tablecloths, hire tables and pay for all the party paraphernalia. Everybody contributed food, cakes and drinks. Rows of tables were set up all along the street and every kid got souvenirs to mark the occasion. The adults bought mugs, so you might get one, and a badge and a flag, everything to match. Some of the stuff is worth something now. Danny's sister Pauline used to collect the mugs and coins and all the royal memorabilia.

There was a live band and all the mums and dads got dressed up. The kids too, as if we were all going to an actual wedding. Properly polished up with shiny shoes. All to sit out in the street basically. For our royal wedding celebration,

we had a horse and carriage and our own royal couple –
Danny's eldest sister, Jackie, was Lady Di and Jerry Judge,
in full military outfit, was Prince Charles. They paraded
along the street in the carriage with everyone cheering. Jerry
Judge had been the star of the Yorkie chocolate bar advert
– the original Yorkie Man. In the advert, he was the truck
driver. But he wasn't just acting the part of a strong, tough
guy, he was the real deal. He set up a security company
and worked with some of the world's biggest stars: Frank
Sinatra, Johnny Depp, Paul McCartney, Arnold
Schwarzenegger, Antonio Banderas, Julia Roberts. He even
made cameo appearances in some of Johnny Depp's films.

Jerry grew up proper tough. He had pitbull dogs he
used to take over to Barnsbury Park. Fearsome dogs. We
kind of knew him and washed his car, an E-Type Jag,
which was a classic even then. It was beautiful and
incredibly fast. A great car, as long as you don't go round
a corner too quickly. I was a budding actor, a wannabe
star, and Jerry was a big character right there on my
doorstep. A giant of a man, well respected in the community. He was married to one of Danny's aunts for a time.
Joanne says he remembered me well because I was such
a cheeky chap.

I went with the Wooders to the Italian procession every
year. It was brilliant. It stemmed from the Italians arriving
in London and becoming part of the community. Every
year they'd celebrate their heritage and the new lives they'd
made. Many started off generations ago in Clerkenwell
and around Exmouth Market, near the City of London.

They also had a base in Hatton Garden market, the jewellery quarter.

They built an Italian church on Farringdon Road. At the back was an open area where the community would meet before the procession all dressed in traditional costume. They'd start off, some of them in the back of open-top vehicles all different sizes, local Italian businesses using their own trucks and vans to parade through the streets. The men would be on the back of the trucks, dressed smartly in black and carrying crosses, with little children in their best clothes on board too. The men would wave, the children sing hymns. The women walked behind dressed in traditional clothes, looking incredible, so beautiful. They also carried crosses. It could have been a scene straight out of Sicily.

Local people would line the streets on both sides as the parade went by. Afterwards, everyone gathered back behind the church. The whole event was somewhere between a religious ceremony, a Lord Mayor's show, a funfair, a street party and a market that represented all aspects of London's vibrant Italian community. There were all sorts of stalls. Some selling a huge range of properly delicious Italian food, as well as clothes, tea towels, and any kind of bric-a-brac you could think of. One year, the funfair had a coconut stall. I won a crazy number of coconuts, at least ten or twelve, and made myself poorly drinking all the water from them. It put me off coconuts for years.

We knew Italians, which was why we were there every year without fail. The Wooders had Italian friends and after the procession they'd join them for a drink and something to eat. A lot of people used to go to Exmouth Market where there were Italian restaurants, especially if they didn't want to be where the crowds were. There was a wine bar with tables outside where Danny's dad and his Italian mates would gather.

As we kids got older, we did our own thing. Maureen couldn't keep track of us because there were so many people but she knew we'd all meet up in the end. When we were hungry, we knew where to find them. There would be a disco later in the day, back in the car park by the church. It was quite an occasion. Everyone dressed to the nines, out for a good time. Families getting together, eating and drinking, dancing. It was brilliant, almost like a royal wedding, Italian style.

10

A Big Adventure

AMERICA SCREAMED THE MOVIES TO ME. IT WAS A BIG deal. Some of Danny's relatives went there and came back with baseball bats, balls and gloves – all that sort of stuff. We would attempt a game of baseball, which was probably just us playing rounders and trying to shout out American stuff we'd heard on TV in our best Hollywood accents. Baseball was something we'd seen in the movies and seemed glamorous. Everything American seemed to ooze glamour to us.

Then, as if by magic, when I was ten years old, we went all the way to a posh Florida resort on a big adventure. It was the holiday of a lifetime that Danny's mum and dad had dreamed of and wanted to experience with the whole family while their kids, even Danny's eldest sisters, were still young. They were kind enough, and crazy enough, to invite me along. This time everything went smoothly at the airport and we were allowed to stay on the plane! It was a long flight, nine or ten hours, but we were so excited, even being on the plane was fun. We probably tired ourselves out and slept through some of it, which would have given Danny's parents a bit of a break.

We landed on the other side of the Atlantic and there we were. In America. I could hardly believe it.

We may have been thousands of miles from home but some things never change and before we'd even got our gear up to the apartment, Danny and I nicked a golf buggy. We couldn't believe they were just lying there in rows waiting to be pinched! We thought maybe that's just how it was there, buggies for everyone. In no time we'd dumped it and took off, running round and round the pool, before we stripped off and jumped in naked, as a bunch of elderly Americans looked on in horror from their deckchairs.

The next day, we took another buggy and drove to the shops. We pulled up in a nicked golf buggy at Larry's Ice Cream Shop, bold as brass. I loved the sound of the name 'Larry's Ice Cream Shop'. It was just so American. We had a few dollars that Maureen had given us and gorged ourselves. Every flavour you could possibly imagine, toppings we had never dreamt of. It was delicious. Probably full of every E number ever invented. Just what me and Danny needed. A massive sugar rush and a load of chemicals.

We decided the decent thing to do was take ice cream back for everyone. We got back into 'our' buggy and drove to the apartment complex with the best intentions. By the time we arrived the ice cream was melting over everything and we managed to dirty up every polished glass door in the complex, leaving behind a sticky mess. It wasn't the great surprise for everyone we'd planned, more a case of, 'What the . . .?' Maureen sent us straight to the bathroom to clean up. What was left of the ice cream cones went straight into the bin.

I'd adapted my party trick with the pint glass and would press my face against a window, open my huge mouth as big as it would go (which was very wide indeed), then blow out my cheeks and pull a kind of cross-eyed funny face. We thought it would be hilarious to sneak up outside people's windows and surprise the old folk sitting inside eating. We assumed they'd find my party trick hilarious too. They didn't.

Soon after, we got a knock on our door and two Americans told Maureen that because of my antics, they had sent for the president. Maureen went pale. 'The president? The president's coming round to have a go at me about the boys, what am I going to do?'

Maureen, who normally took everything in her stride and saw the funny side of any situation, started shouting, 'I'm never taking you two anywhere again. You create havoc wherever you go. Now we're all going to be thrown out of the country.' She immediately began cleaning the floor in preparation for the president's arrival.

The only time me and Danny had ever heard of 'the president' was when it was about the actual President of the United States of America, so we were thinking Ronald Reagan, who was president then, was on his way. Had we really been so bad that they were actually sending Ronald Reagan to throw us out of the country when we'd only just arrived?!

We expected a limo at any moment with police and security and everything. Then a little man turned up at the door on his own, no fanfare, no police escort. He was the president of the apartment block, he explained. Whatever Maureen said must have worked because we all got to stay. Maybe it was the spotless floor that did it.

Florida really did look like something out of the movies. The big apartment block we were staying in resembled a block of flats but to us was way posher because it was right on the beach. The beach was nothing like the ones we were used to, where the weather was a bit of a gamble, even in the summer. This was proper sunny sunshine all the time. Palm trees everywhere and everything seemed so clean. Before we got to it, anyway.

There was an aura of luxury about everything and Florida was as bright and colourful as back home could be dark and gloomy. It felt like all things were on a bigger scale, from the ice creams to the cars, which were identical to the ones on the American cop shows, strangely enough. They were massive. Some of those proper old 1970s gas guzzlers were still about, with V8 engines that actually gurgled as they drove past – a totally different sound to a Morris Marina. The bonnets that housed these monster engines were about the length of a typical British family car. The biggest cars we'd been in before were the likes of Danny's dad's, but for the first time even that seemed small in comparison. None of this 'bigger is better' obsession was doing the climate many favours but we were kids and were like 'wow' everywhere we looked, walking round open-mouthed at it all. A case of total sensory overload at how exotic everything was.

Within a day or so, we had made friends with some neighbouring holidaymakers. The dads were into their fishing and seemed to have trained their whole families up. Someone got a load of extra equipment from somewhere and invited us along and showed us how to fish properly with rods and all the gear. We went down to a pier, a docks area, where we could look out to sea and do some serious fishing.

We caught loads of fish, mainly catfish, barracuda too. This was seriously exciting and wildly exotic compared with the fucking stickleback I used to catch down in the Regent's Canal when I was a kid with an old bit of netting. This was a whole new type of fishing, learning how to use a rod and line properly. It was a proper skill. A sport. We didn't eat the fish. We learned how to take the hook out without harming them and threw them back so they could swim away. It was exciting to see what fish we could catch, how big they were, what they looked like close up. Even though I found it calming sitting on the dock waiting for a bite, it was exciting as well, mainly because there were so many fish. If I hadn't caught anything I wouldn't have lasted five minutes.

At night, we sometimes went to the shopping mall. One time I wanted perfume. I was with Maureen and I told her I wanted to buy something for my aunt. I knew I had to go back to Stonefield Street after the holiday and thought that maybe things wouldn't be so bad if I took Carol something she liked. I think I also wanted to find a scent like the one my mum used to wear. Maureen left me with the saleswoman while she checked something on the next counter. I got the poor woman to get every perfume out of a cupboard and line them up on the counter. I smelled them all. None of them smelled like the one I remember my mum had. So in the end, I walked away, having bought nothing, leaving the saleswoman with a counter strewn with perfume bottles. She had to put the whole lot back again. I was a nightmare.

On another shopping trip, Maureen twigged that me and Danny had a scam going nicking trainers. She still talks about it now, the moment she spotted Danny putting his old trainers on the shelf in the shop and walking out in the brand-new ones he had been trying on. Maureen remembers thinking, 'We've got to get out, we're going to end up in prison here.' She got hold of us both and slapped us round the head, shouting, 'I can't be having this, I can't be doing this no more. You're the worst two boys put together.' It wasn't the first time we'd heard her say that and I can't deny it was horribly true.

The Florida trip was an amazing adventure. And we didn't always cause havoc. A lot of the time we did but not always. I was so lucky to be invited. Maureen was so tolerant. She had the patience of a saint. I have no idea how she put up with me, other than that she knew I genuinely loved her and her family. Joanne says people loved me because I was naughty but nice, though I was always getting up to mischief. Joanne put up with a lot too. One time I accidentally hit her on the head with a golf club and nearly knocked her out. She still loved me!

11

A Petty Thief

I GOT ARRESTED WHEN I WAS ONLY TEN WHEN, ALONG
with a friend, I broke into the school. The police turned
up at home because someone had seen us and knew who
we were. That really put the wind up me. I had to report
at the police station and it was clear what a big deal that
was, which shook me up a bit. I hadn't looked at what I
was doing as risky, thinking it was just a bit of fun.

When we got in through the school skylight, we didn't
even know what we were going to nick, just thought we'd
take whatever we found. Then we saw bikes and thought
we'd get them and some sweets and cycle away. We forgot
how tricky it would be to climb over the fence with the
bikes but, somehow, we managed. My accomplice was a
kid two doors up and he was only nine, too young to be

cautioned or anything. At the police station I was told, 'This is a formal warning and if you do anything like this again, we'll throw the book at you.'

The police coming to the door and having to report at the station so they could keep a check on me, make sure I was behaving, gave me the creeps good and proper. I think my aunt encouraged them to take a tough line because she was worried about me. She didn't want me, or Scott, to go down the same road as our eldest brothers, realizing they were going to land in serious trouble one day. It hit home that if I did anything like that again I'd be going to borstal, taken away from everyone and everything I knew. I thought, 'Shit.' Suddenly it became horribly real and didn't seem much like fun.

From then on, any thieving I did was petty. No more break-ins. My career as a cat burglar was over at the tender age of ten. Thieving was an adrenaline rush. I'd get scared but I had a kind of addiction. Kleptomania, almost. From then on, I kept to stuff I knew I could handle – shoplifting. Nothing criminal beyond that. Somehow, I managed not get caught, didn't have security guards running after me or anything. I happened to be very good at it.

We started going 'up West' – what Londoners call going to the West End – me, Danny and Joanne. We'd get our red rover bus ticket and head off. Although we were allowed to play out we were supposed to stay near the house. We certainly weren't allowed to jump on a bus. Neither Carol nor Maureen knew what we were up to.

In Russell Square, there was a big fountain and in

summer we would run in and out of it, getting totally soaked. We'd go to the British Museum and run riot. We played 'run outs', which was a bit like a rowdy version of hide and seek. Someone was 'it' and you had to tag each other. There we were, running around crazy in the British Museum. Danny and Joanne's big sister, Pauline, used to get really pissed off because when she tried to go to the museum the guards would associate her with us and turn her away. Funnily enough, we probably learnt a lot from our visits. When we did history at school, or went out for museum days, I would be able to pinpoint where things were because of playing run outs there.

Sometimes we wandered round the shops. Hamleys, the toy shop on Regent Street, C&A, Selfridges, Harrods. We'd go to all of the big stores and, given an opportunity, would take something. Me and Danny, anyway. Not Joanne, who was a good girl and didn't get involved with any of that carry-on. In C&A, I would grab a ski jacket because they were by the fire exits, at the bottom of the stairwell. I'd put a ski jacket on and walk out. It was a good scam.

Those trips gave us a sense of a completely different London to the one we'd grown up in. Our world was council flats and the market, then suddenly we were wandering around Harrods looking at stuff we couldn't afford. It didn't bother us because we'd help ourselves anyway.

When adults talked about going 'up West' it was like, 'Ooh. All a bit posh, the West End.' Like saying, 'I've got money. I'm gonna spend some.' For kids like us, it was an illicit adventure. It was always buzzing, full of people. The hustle and bustle felt exciting.

Me and Danny were both into clothes – Benetton, Ralph Lauren. We'd clean cars to earn a bit of money, duck and dive, and I'd get a bit from the acting jobs I was doing. Our favourite shop was Benetton, on South Molton Street. The United Colours of Benetton adverts were famous. Colourful clothes, omnicultural models. There was a kind of rugby top that was quite well known with 0-12 Benetton on it. If you had one of them you were a rich kid. You definitely wouldn't expect to see them on kids from our background. So we'd come back from our trips up West and walk up and down with our rich kid Benetton rugby tops on.

We liked Lacoste. They were the first designer clothes we were aware of. And we loved Fila tracksuits. It was starting to be a status symbol, a mark of honour on the street, to have an expensive designer tracksuit. We'd generally have to buy them, though we managed to nick one or two. Lacoste was in South Molton Street too so that was a real destination for us even when we were as young as ten or eleven. The area around Bond Street had always been the hub for designers and we were in this super wealthy zone where all the exclusive shops were, even though we weren't from a rich background.

From what I've seen, most people who haven't got wealth but come into money want to show it off at the first opportunity. But having a sports car or nice clothes doesn't necessarily mean you're rich. In a way, all we had was ourselves and the clothes we stood up in. We didn't really have money. I lived in a council flat. But we could go into a wealthy part of town that was just a bus ride away from our patch and enter a completely different world that reeked of wealth. Glamour and flash cars everywhere. Brand new Porches and Ferraris and limos. Not a second-hand Capri Ghia in sight.

I thought, if I can nick, or buy, the kind of clothes a rich kid would wear then I'll look like a rich kid and I might even feel like a rich kid. It was all superficial. Whether or not I had money I wanted to look as good as I could. It was all I could do. I didn't have the huge house and fancy car. I didn't go to a posh school and speak with the right accent. But perhaps I could look as good as anyone . . .

I couldn't nick everything. Sometimes I had to pay for things I wanted. In the more expensive shops the clothes were tagged so it was hard to shoplift. We could never wander round now nicking things the way we used to. Even in the cheaper shops there are security cameras everywhere. In our day, there would sometimes be a single security person for the whole place and they couldn't be everywhere at once.

The more I got into acting the less I shoplifted, until it pretty much stopped altogether. I knew I didn't want to go down that particular road because I had a good idea where it would lead.

I was a massive James Bond fan. They were the first proper action films, big on glitz and glamour with those amazing stunts. Then there was the great music – theme tunes that were hits. I would get completely lost in those films; I could watch them over and over and never get bored.

My Bond actor growing up was mainly Roger Moore. I liked Sean Connery as well, though his stint in the starring role, apart from one later appearance in *Never Say Never Again*, ended just before I was born, but we'd see his films on the repeats on the telly. The stunts really intrigued me. Even when I first started getting into Bond movies when I was eight or nine, I always wanted to know how they did them and I used to try and do my own, with just a pedal bike. I'd also fall down the stairs, playing at being a stuntman. As a little kid, I could tumble down a flight of stairs and roll and roll and not get hurt.

I was so obsessed with the Bond movies that I spent ages trying to memorize the scenes and the lines. I'd almost re-enact an entire Bond movie in my head, doing my own stunts, being Bond and the baddy and the stunt guy. If I found out a Bond was going to be shown on telly I'd have to watch. We knew there would always be one guaranteed over Christmas.

I was also a fan of old Mickey Rooney films from an early age. I'd watch everything of his on TV. Rooney was a real all-rounder. He could act, sing and dance. He'd been a child star and I suppose that was inspiring for me, as I was already acting and Mickey Rooney was small, like me.

Then, of course, there was my complete obsession with *Bugsy Malone*. It was the first film I got on video and I played it hundreds of times. I went through a phase where every day when I got home from school it went on. I was so into it and really taken with the idea that one of the Anna Scher kids, Dexter Fletcher, was actually in it. One of the things I loved was the song at the end of the film: 'We could have been anything that we wanted to be.' It was a sentiment that was drummed into us at drama school and really resonated with me.

Each year, I would get three or four smallish jobs, building up into slightly bigger opportunities. I did film and TV, BBC plays, period drama, mostly uncredited. Some more prestigious than others. A particularly good BBC one was about the legendary explorer, Sir Ernest Shackleton. Originally called *Shackleton*, it was subsequently renamed *Icebound in the Antarctic*. When I was twelve I had a small part in a pretty awful ITV sitcom called *Bottle Boys*, starring Robin Askwith of the infamously smutty 1970s Confessions films. Then there were some skits on live TV that I developed through improvisation, which I'm still proud of. Me and some other kids did a whole series called 'No Adults Allowed' on the then new *TV-am*. I was so hyper on that job that they banned me from eating sweets. They used to give them to me at the end, once the job was done, so I could go berserk somewhere else.

I started to get quite busy with the TV work but there were restrictions on how many days child actors could officially take out of school, even though I was taking plenty of unofficial ones. At one point, I'd used up all my allotted out-of-school days and was being offered jobs I wasn't allowed to take, which was annoying. I was flavour of the month, teacher's pet in my drama group. Anna Scher loved me. There were certain people in class she particularly liked and I was definitely one of them. She could probably see I was made for all the scruffy urchin, Artful Dodgery-type roles. I mean, I wasn't exactly your typical little drama school kid and Anna knew that.

A whole different side of me was developing at drama school, in tandem with my messed-up street kid side. Sometimes it was difficult to balance the two. Once the messed-up kid in me came out of nowhere and I started fighting someone in my acting class. In time, I got better at channelling everything into acting. I was a bright kid. My IQ is surprisingly high – quite ironic, especially considering the role that made me famous; Ricky isn't exactly known as the brains of Albert Square! This hyperactive mind of mine had to be used, had to be challenged. I had to do something. Most of what we did at drama school was improvisation-based, so I could swear, shout, really go for it. There was a lot of shouting and screaming – probably a very useful release and ideal training for *EastEnders*, really. Whenever I was acting, I felt a sense of being another person, which was cathartic. I could step into a different world, be someone else – at least for a while – and get away from my life.

12

Fight!

GREAT TRACTS OF WASTELAND WERE OPENING UP IN
Islington as flats were demolished. They cleared a big area
near me. Years later, they built a giant Sainsbury's on it
and a car park where the Spanish Pats used to be. The
open space brought travellers into the area, with their
fairgrounds, horses, trailers, the lot. They didn't live in the
old painted wagons, they had modern caravans, and the
families were Irish. There were lots of second- and
third-generation Irish in Islington at the time as well as
more recent immigrants. But people seemed to hate the
travellers, or at least be suspicious, whatever background
they were from themselves. It was like everyone was scared
of them. And things could turn nasty. A mate of mine had

a run-in he's never forgotten. He was ten, on the swings behind St Stephen's church.

There were three swings in a row – two of them empty and my mate was on the other one. A little kid came over. He was only about six years old and had been sent by two older brothers, aged about thirteen or fourteen. The kid said, 'Get off the swing,' and my mate was like, 'Get on another one.' The kid said, 'I want that swing,' and my mate went, 'Fuck off, get on one of them other ones.' This carried on, the kid telling my mate, 'You better fucking get off.'

Then he walked away back to his brothers, had a little conversation and came back again. 'Get off the swing,' he said.

My mate wouldn't budge and then . . . BOOM! He thought the kid had punched him in the leg. The kid turned and went back to his brothers. My mate looked down to see blood pouring through his jeans. He had been stabbed. It didn't even hurt when it happened but the minute he saw blood it was like, 'Whooooaah!' He ran screaming to his mum, she went steaming over and slapped the little kid into the middle of next week. His brothers shit it and ran away. If the kid thought he was going to get protected by his brothers, was he fuck! Then my mate's mum rushed him off to get fixed up. It wasn't a proper knife or anything, thank fuck, I think it was a dart, though that was bad enough.

My brother Darren, when I was about eleven years old, would, almost as a bet, force me to go and fight the

Sid's mum (Joanie) holding Sid. Scott (bottom left), Darren (bottom right), with a friend. Sid's dad, who was standing behind Scott, was scratched out of the photograph in the 1970s

Darren, Scott and Sid, taken when Sid was about five

Messing around
as a kid

Sid with Aunt Flossie

Sid (left) with a fellow cast member, filming *Shackleton* for BBC Two in 1983, aged eleven

Locked up

At a birthday party for a school friend, aged seven or eight

The old basement council flat (*left*) where Sid used to live; the street has changed a lot over the years

Danny, Joanne and Sid 'holding the table' for the adults at the clubhouse, Clacton-on-Sea

First year at Highbury Grove secondary school

(*below*) Peter Gordon and Ashley, Sid and Joanne – temporarily boyfriend and girlfriend
(*right*) Danny and Sid at the entrance to the clubhouse

(*left*) Sid getting ready to box with Danny in the front room at the Wooder's house
(*below*) Sid in Florida, play-acting

Sid's 40th Birthday @ Gilgamesh

Sid with Maureen and Danny Wooder (senior). The Woilders are still a part of Sid's life today

(*below left*) Sid, Danny, Joanne and a friend at the Italian procession in 1982
(*below right*) Sid at Southbank, late 1985; nearly fourteen

Filming *Revolution* with
Al Pacino

On the set of *EastEnders*

Sid's on-screen family – father Frank (Mike Reid), step-mum Pat (Pam St Clement), and sister Diane (Sophie Lawrence)

travellers. I had no choice or Darren would beat me up more than the gypsy kid would. It seems harsh but Darren was always wanting to toughen me up. He put me up for fights with loads of kids. I was small for my age and he thought I'd be too vulnerable if I couldn't fight. He wanted me to be a proper scrapper and was proud of me when I was. I hated it but he insisted it was for my own good.

The word would spread around like wildfire if a fight was going to happen. It's amazing how much word of mouth there was, when that was all kids had. By the time it came to the fight, at whatever place had been arranged, a circle of kids would already be waiting and as you entered the ring, chants of 'fight, fight, fight, fight' would get louder and louder. Your adrenaline builds up beforehand along with that nervous feeling in your tummy. You'd try not to be scared. You'd definitely try to never look scared, even if you were. You'd try not to cry, even if you got beaten up. They put their kids in our school, so I used to have fights there as well, so it wasn't just Darren setting stuff up.

It must have been tough for the gypsy kids. Fighting seemed to be the only way some of the kids from the estates ever communicated with them. Me, Danny and Joanne started to hang out with them and we became friends.

That was when we got into motorbikes, even though we were almost too small for even the smallest kids' bike. Eddie Kidd, the motorcyclist, lived locally and he was a bit of hero for us, which must have been an influence. The gypsy kids had bikes and we were desperate for shots on them. We couldn't wait to get on them and try stunts.

There was a real thing about young kids doing trail biking then and even a kids' TV programme about it called *Kick Start*, presented by Peter Purves from *Blue Peter*. The whole show was basically footage of young kids going up and down steep trails and doing stunts and stuff. Luckily having all that waste ground around us meant there were plenty of old planks and bricks lying around – we used to build ramps in Stonefield Street, then bring them to where the caravans were because there was a great rough area at the back, ideal for scrambling. We'd have fights there too, even after we'd made friends with the kids who lived there. It was mostly fun, but sometimes serious, and sometimes I still had to fight them properly when Darren put me up for it.

We were street rogues really, hanging round and causing havoc.

After primary school, I went to Highbury Grove. Darren's reputation in primary school meant that no one would fuck with me, or Scott either, even after he left. But Darren went to Holloway Comprehensive because it was closer to where he stayed with his Aunt Grace and so the sense of being protected by him changed when I went to Highbury Grove – in fact, it was the reverse. Now I was no one. A very small fish in a big, rough comprehensive. Now the tough kids had brothers that were older than Darren, bigger than him and some were even harder. The worst thing was that they had something to prove. It was proper terrifying, coming up from primary school at eleven years old, once they heard I was from a family of fighters. Like a gunslinger coming to town in some old cowboy movie.

The school had a 'house' system with posh sounding names. Marlborough, Richmond, Gloucester, Bedford, Oxford, York. Every kid was allocated a house. Some bright spark of a head teacher had probably found it was a great system for building team spirit and friendly rivalry at bloody Eton or somewhere. The kids at Highbury Grove saw it as a great system for organizing fights. We wouldn't fight with kids in the same house though, so maybe the team spirit bit worked out, though the rivalry didn't seem too friendly when you were getting a kicking.

Because of my background, every wannabe hard nut in every other house wanted a go. It was a nightmare. Thankfully, there was a big guy called Gibberall in my house. Absolutely no one would fuck with Gibberall. I was little as a kid and he was twice the size of me, even though we were the same age. He was in my class and I got on with him, so we became friends, which protected me to some extent.

One time though, I had to fight a guy from Marlborough house. Everyone was standing round watching. A proper knuckle fight. He tried to rip my mouth open – put his fingers in and yanked. I instinctively bit him, taking one of his fingers clean off. I didn't realize what I'd done, I just knew I'd won the fight as he screamed and ran off, clutching his hand, blood spouting all over the place. He went to hospital and they sewed his finger back on. That night, his parents turned up at my uncle and aunt's door with him in tow, a huge bandage on his finger, saying, 'Look what you've done!' After that, everyone started calling me 'dog'. I got taunted and bullied for that for a bit. I'd sort of got trapped in my own reputation.

There were also fights between Highbury Grove and Islington Green schools. My friend John, who went to Islington Green in the same era as I was at Highbury Grove, has some great anecdotes from the other side! John reckons to call them 'fights' is probably overrating the contribution of Islington Green. It has to be said, they did take a few slaps. He also remembers playing us at football, when they usually lost, with scores like 10–2 to us, though, to be fair, we weren't too fussy about any rules. John says, 'We'd be fielding under-elevens and half the other team seemed to have moustaches.'

One time there was a 'grudge fight' at St Mary's church-yard, just behind Upper Street, between the schools. Islington Green turned up with some of the hardest kids from their school, about thirty of them. I think they thought they might actually win a fight for once, because there were three times as many of them. We were just first years, eleven and twelve years old, more there to stand at the edge to watch rather than really have a go.

Anyway, the churchyard had old painted metal railings. The ones that have a long, high strip with holes in, where long poles had been put through. Poles with spikes at the top, to stop people climbing over. As soon as word got back that things might be unevenly matched, our lot started booting the sides of the railings and sliding out the poles. Within a few minutes, they were armed with bloody great spears and started to charge. John says, 'All thirty of us turned and ran from the ten psychopaths from Highbury Grove.'

Football hooligans would set up a fight with one school against another. And when it involved Holloway Comprehensive, who would be the one leading the school and up the front? Darren. That's the sort of thing we were growing up with, so everyone was aware of how fucking tough Darren was and I found myself in a bit of a corner. I started to feel frightened a lot of the time. Even if I was getting a beating Darren would punch me, like, 'Get back in there!' He wouldn't let me lose so I had no choice. Pretty much all kids want to impress their peers and be like them – that's all you know. But you get a reputation and you become trapped.

I had Anna Scher's of course to keep me out of trouble at least some of the time. And I made friends with some of the middle-class kids there who showed me that there was another world apart from the way of life I knew. But it wasn't just drama school, there were other things that we could go to that gave us some sort of structure or even discipline. There were church clubs that would let me in to play football and various youth clubs too. Even though Darren was no angel, he'd got himself properly christened, as a fourteen-year-old, to get more involved in the club. There was the boxing club on White Lion Street, too. We did all that stuff.

I've been back and looked in at some of the places I

used to go as a child. I'm not a member of any particular religion but I appreciate what the churches did for me and other kids. They tried their best to help. The combination of Anna Scher and the church showed me a side of life I would never otherwise have seen. They say that if your dad's been in prison, the likelihood of you going to prison is much higher, and when you've grown up with family who've been in and out the nick, like it's an occupational hazard, it's pretty hard to be one of the only ones who doesn't end up inside. If I'd not kept going with the acting, I would have been a jailbird the rest of my life. Absolutely 100 per cent.

13

Up the Arsenal

FOOTBALL WAS A HUGE PART OF ISLINGTON LIFE. THE Wooders are all Tottenham Hotspur fans and I'm Arsenal. As a kid, Danny never stopped reminding me their dad had told them that Arsenal were originally from Woolwich in south London. That's why they're called the Woolwich Gunners. I was bigger than him so every time he said it he'd get beaten up. We grew up loving each other but hating each other's teams at the same time. It's crazy really. Danny's still mad for Spurs. I still think my favourite Gunners player of all time is Liam Brady.

Arsenal tended to have the most support round our way, especially with the old Highbury ground being just up the road. Spurs – based just a few miles north – were our deadly rivals. There were four pubs, one on each corner, at Barnsbury park, just down from Chapel Market. Three of them were Arsenal and one was Tottenham. As you'd imagine.

Most kids were born into a Gunners or Spurs family and the support went down through the generations. Some brave kids chose a team from outside the area. Some even came from a 'mixed marriage' – one parent an Arsenal fan, the other Tottenham! We had neighbours where the older son became a Tottenham fan, much to the delight of his dad's side of the family who were die-hard Spurs. Then the younger brother chose Arsenal. His uncles on his dad's side were really put out. 'If you're going to be an Arsenal fan you won't get any more presents from us,' they said. Every Christmas, they'd shower the older brother with presents while the younger one got a Curly Wurly.

Our family are Arsenal through and through. My brothers Darren and Scott in particular. Arsenal mad. They got that from their dad, even though he was in the nick most of the time when they grew up. Darren especially remembers that bit of family life with him.

We used to love the chants at Highbury in the eighties. Darren and Scott would dine out on it forever if they managed to start a chant on the north bank that the whole stadium sang. If you were playing someone who wasn't very good you'd sing, 'Are you watching Tottenham?' Or 'Are you Tottenham in disguise?'

I didn't get to go to a lot of away games but I do remember people would go on the Arsenal train – wives and whole families included. We know a guy whose mum took him to his first away game at Leeds when he was about ten. He remembers getting to Kings Cross Station and being told which carriage of the train to get into. A big guy on the door told his mum, 'Don't worry, Madam, the Arsenal will look after you.'

For the journey, Arsenal ladies would prepare rolls. They were usually those slimming Energen rolls, round and crunchy with a dry texture, and filled with ham or cheese. They'd be in bags and anyone could help themselves, you didn't have to pay.

When they got to Leeds, there was a police escort on horseback to take them from the station to the ground at Elland Road. They were moved along to the bit of the stadium for away fans. They watched the game and came back. John and his mum got season tickets after that and became regulars at both home and away games. John said that there were two women, a mother and daughter, who were always on the supporters' train, wherever the game was. The daughter must have been in her sixties and the mother in her eighties. They would take a flask of tea and pass it round to everyone, making sure Islington's community spirit went with the Arsenal fans.

Everyone loved the home games. The old Arsenal stadium, Highbury, was awesome. It was surrounded by houses and some people could see in from their bedrooms. Inside the ground, you were so near the pitch. So near the players. If you sat in the upper east stand it had its own independent staircase.

The tube station there was something else with gates up the middle and wire fencing. Even on a normal non-match day, at busy times it felt like you were being herded like sheep, or prisoners in Alcatraz. It's all still there, even though Arsenal don't play there any more and they've built a load of flats where the pitch was.

It was exciting going to the old terraces as a kid. Scott was a serious football fan and would sometimes let me tag along with him and his pals. He was so into it all that I fed off his enthusiasm. The feeling of being part of something great was immense. It was just part of us, even for people that weren't obsessed with it. You couldn't really ignore it. Back in our bit of Islington, if the wind was in the right direction you could hear the crowd, so when Arsenal scored and a roar went up the whole of Islington would explode. It was part of the identity of living there. When Arsenal won there would be chant after chant. Not many places have a football stadium in the middle of the community.

Having the stadium in the heart of the area was something we were all proud of. It made us feel good, superior in a way. You could walk to it across Highbury Fields. It looked old fashioned and at the same time impressive as you approached the Art Deco entrance. The building itself was beautiful. Highbury was always crowded but didn't feel threatening. As soon as the rule on standing changed and everywhere had to have seats the atmosphere changed but it was still great. The players' dressing room was across the street, on Avenell Road, and if we won we went round there and the players would come out and wave at us.

The connection between Islington and Arsenal was powerful but there were kids in every class at school who came from a family that supported another team. Mostly the big rivals, Tottenham, like Danny's family, but others who'd decided to support teams like Liverpool, who seemed a bit glamourous. Glory hunters, we called them! It was great giving them stick when their team started slipping. To be fair, choosing a team other than Arsenal was one way of striving for individuality and I'm all for that, so I had a bit of grudging respect. Though my brothers would have gone completely mental if I'd tried striving for individuality that way, so just as well I had the acting. In our family, Arsenal were sacred. We knew a kid who went Everton, just to wind up the smug Liverpool fans. He chose well because Everton then had a great run.

The local derby games were massive. If Arsenal won it was the best feeling in the world. If Tottenham beat Arsenal these days, I almost want to turn my phone off, because the abuse will flow, especially from a Spurs friend, like Danny!

Back then Arsenal really didn't respect Tottenham. That changed recently. In the past, the chant was always something insulting about the mother of whoever the Tottenham manager was. They don't really do that since Pochettino managed Spurs. He changed things. The whole rivalry thing has become much more respectful.

There was talk of Arsenal sharing Wembley, which would

have been a total nightmare – it's absolutely miles away, for a start. Then there was a surveyor, who later became a vicar, who said, 'Look there's a space by the railway tracks. That's where Arsenal should build.' They were going to have to move some businesses to make it happen. The leader of the council was a football fan, so he supported it. They could see the point commercially, with people flocking to the area. Spending money. Arsenal needed to stay around Islington and the new site wasn't that far away. Still, the move to the Emirates was emotional. We loved Highbury. Grown men cried on the last day there. It felt like the end of an era. The atmosphere on Avenell Road was extraordinary, a one-off. We knew it wouldn't be the same anywhere else.

I would play football on Highbury Fields, everyone just turning up to have a game. If it rained too much and got seriously muddy, one of the older kids would go, 'Let's go up to the Arsenal,' and we'd head off with the older boys and talk about Arsenal v Tottenham.

Sometimes our path would cross with Spurs fans, which could get a bit tasty. It was when you got a little bit older that someone might whack you. If you were younger than eleven or twelve you could virtually sit within touching distance of two groups of teenagers and watch them beating the living shit out of each other without getting dragged into it!

There was hardly any trouble on match day unless it was a Tottenham game, or maybe Millwall. In the late 1970s and early '80s the ultra-right National Front tried to use football rivalry to drive a wedge between supporters. Spurs had become known as having quite a lot of Jewish support, so the NF thought Arsenal fans might be good fodder for recruiting, hoping to stir up anti-Semitism. But we'd always had black fans and black players and, while probably not a lot of the hardcore Arsenal fans were Jewish, they had Jewish friends and neighbours, some of whom were Arsenal supporters. Despite Arsenal's legendary rivalry with Tottenham, the idea that we could be split along racial or religious lines was always nonsense.

The ridiculous thing was that the NF started trying to recruit outside the old Spurs ground, White Hart Lane, as well as outside our ground. The teams would be at home on alternate Saturdays so the same National Front people went from one ground to the other every weekend handing out far-right fascist flyers.

Around the early eighties, there was a proper backlash against NF trying to recruit Arsenal and handing out pamphlets. The top guy in the Arsenal firm was called Denton – also known as the Bear. He was big and black and hard as fuck. Denton managed to come to a kind of agreement with the Spurs firm. Generally, they'd quite happily beat the shit out of each other but one thing they didn't want was NF fuckers handing out their pamphlets at Highbury. Denton got the Spurs guys onside and the NF Nazi skinheads got the shit kicked out of them by the Arsenal and Tottenham firms working together, which you would have thought would never happen. Then the NF thought they'd be clever and send down some old guys to hand out the pamphlets, thinking they'd be safe. They were properly scared off as well and their pamphlets thrown in the canal. In the end, the NF were driven out and forced to spread their poison elsewhere. For all the intense rivalry between Tottenham and Arsenal, they had managed to form an unlikely bond on that particular issue.

14

Changes

WHEN YOU CROSSED OVER CALEDONIAN ROAD, TO THE west of us, it was mostly council estates and that's where it really started to get rough. Anything really hairy usually happened over there, or the estate kids crossed the road over to our bit and started stuff. They've now completely redeveloped that part of Kings Cross but around there, especially north of Kings Cross station, used to be notorious.

You had the scrag end of estates, old derelict buildings and acres upon acres of waste ground where there used to be huge industrial sites or slums. You can just imagine all the little street urchins running round using the place as a playground. At the back of the Anna Sher school on Matilda Street there was a factory that shut down and kids used to climb onto Anna's roof and play down on the rail track. It was properly dangerous!

We used to head down to the canal, where we would mix with kids from the estates and dare each other to jump in and swim to the other side. I couldn't tell you how many times we swam across that canal, not for a second stopping to think how dangerous it was! It was filthy but at that age we didn't care. So much of the waste ground we played on has become home to poshed-up developments now, although they've incorporated as many bits of historical architecture as they could that were derelict in our day, like closed-down factories, as people seem to like that sort of stuff now.

As a laugh, Danny's sister Jackie would pick us up in the car and take us prostitute spotting! They'd hang around on Shirley Street (which doesn't exist now) and Goods Way, near Kings Cross station. Jackie used to call them over and pretend she wanted to speak to them, and then there would be us two little kids in the car jeering. We'd drive off quickly before they killed us. We'd also go down York Way, spotting the men in their cars picking up the prostitutes and we'd beep them and wave and laugh. It would be a kick for us and shameful for them, I guess. Looking back, it was a really bad thing to do.

As soon as Pauline was old enough to drive she was desperate to pass her test and so she got a job and bought an old car, which she picked up cheap. In Islington back then, you didn't have to pay for parking and there was no congestion charge either. As soon as you could, you tried to find a way to drive. People drove without a license all the time. Pauline would drive to work listening to the Highway Code on tape. She then loaned it out for £1 a month, which was very enterprising. It was on a compact cassette and her friends would borrow it to help them pass, even though any of them who could get hold of a car were all driving without a licence as well! It was a musical version of the Highway Code, if you can imagine that, and somehow hearing it sung was a way of learning it really quickly. You only got asked four questions about the Highway Code when you did your test in those days but they could be from anywhere in the book so you had to know it all.

By the early 1980s, the streets were strewn with syringes and glue bags. There were glue sniffers on the streets, especially the side streets. Used condoms laying around the place, just off Copenhagen Street, Liverpool Road and Upper Street though not so much Caledonian Road because that was still busy with blocks of flats and other housing.

A lot was changing in Islington. In 1979, Margaret Thatcher gave council house tenants the right to buy their homes and the Wooders bought theirs for thirty grand at the start of the 1980s, which was quite a lot for them, but the house was big. Later they moved out to a quiet cul de sac in Essex. Everything about it is immaculate, even the garden. Not a blade of grass out of place. Maureen still says she misses Islington but Danny's dad doesn't. It's not his Islington now, he says, even though they'd have been sitting on a goldmine if they'd stayed in their old house. It would be worth millions now. Ex-council tenants who'd had the right to buy started selling up for more and more money. Thanks to 'right to buy', local people quickly wised up to the fact that a council tenancy in Islington could be a valuable asset.

The right to buy was one of the reasons it was becoming harder to get a council flat. Local people couldn't get one even if their parents were council tenants. They could get a place out in Milton Keynes or somewhere but you'd have to go on the list forever to get a flat in Islington. At one time, you'd get generations of families living near one another but that was starting to change. The sense of community was still strong, though. We knew our neighbours. If someone was in trouble everybody rallied round to help, that was how it was. Lots of people didn't have a phone at home. It wasn't until after they moved to Matilda Street that the Wooders got one. Up until then, like most people, they'd knock on someone's door and ask to use theirs. Even late at night, people would tap on a neighbour's window and say, 'Can I use your phone?'

I remember Pauline Wooder got a job working in the dry-cleaners, and for some reason it had a phone. People would come in and use it. She was so nice, she wouldn't say no, though one day we came in and they'd changed it to a kind of mini payphone, so no more free calls for us – and a very relieved Pauline.

CHANGES

Danny's dad was the first person in our area to have a new Mercedes. Everyone else we knew, apart from the few well-to-do people in the big houses, had a rusty Ford Cortina, if they were lucky. He even had a car phone, which was ahead of its time. Most people had only ever seen them in James Bond films, not in real life. The Wooders might not have been rich by everyone's standards, perhaps, but within our culture they were wealthy.

You can still buy classic cars from the late seventies and eighties with a console and a great big, and now totally useless, phone in the middle of it. More like an old house phone, complete with twirly flex, than the mobiles we're now used to. You could drive along talking on your great big phone (legal then) paying an absolute fortune to make calls. I think you could connect to landlines as well as other car phones. I hope so, anyway, as I don't think Danny's dad knew anyone else with a phone in their car. I don't remember him ever using his. It just sat there. For show. On the very rare occasions we were allowed in his car, rather than the van, I hoped it would ring and some big deal would be discussed but it never did.

It's difficult to describe to today's generation of kids how amazing it seemed to us have a phone that wasn't tied to a wall in the house or in a phone box. It was only later that mobile phones came in and then it was only rich, or wannabe rich, yuppie types that had them. They were huge bricks of things with battery packs about twenty times the size of a modern smart phone and were the subject of satire in the 1980s.

Danny's dad was involved in various businesses, not unlike Arthur Daley in the classic TV series *Minder*. Come to think if it, I reckon Arthur Daley had a car phone in his flash car. It was absolutely the thing to have a flash car round our way if you'd done well in business. No one would believe you were doing well if you didn't have the right car. Some guys lived in humble houses, in terraced back streets, but outside would be a flashy motor, often with a bonnet longer than the front of the house. If you were well connected and respected, no one would touch it. Local kids, like us, who would think nothing of robbing anything they could from Tesco, would treat a local flash car with respect. Everyone knew who had what and it was big news if someone changed their car.

Danny's dad always had good music on in his car. Motown and soul, mainly. It must have been something like an old Smooth FM type radio station he tuned into. The tunes he had belting out always made me feel good.

I remember the day he swapped his big Merc for a Range Rover. That was becoming the thing then. The Range evolved from being a car for the county set to a car for the urban businessman. I remember our first drive to Clacton in this huge thing. I think it was the first one with four passenger doors. Danny used to sit at the front in the middle, on the arm rest. No one seemed to bother with seatbelts. We were all set for a trip to the caravan, very excited to be off. Then a huge stone chip flew up and smashed the windscreen and took the edge off things.

Arsenal were playing Tottenham that day too and it was total mayhem.

When I was a kid, there were still plenty of what I call proper old Islington people about who were born in the 1920s. They'd grown up so poor their mothers would save old flour sacks and boil them until they were soft so they could make them into night clothes. Often, the men were dependent on their wives. It was common among elderly couples that if the wife passed away the husband went soon after, sometimes within a few days.

A woman I know, Margaret, who's done a lot for the community, has lived in Islington since the 1970s and knows it like the back of her hand. She grew up outside London, on a council estate, but somewhere a lot quieter so she was a bit more sheltered. She's got a story about her dad driving them up to visit family in Islington at the start of the 1960s. She had one aunt who lived in Gray's Inn Road and another in Canonbury. She remembers sitting in the back seat of a little Austin, staring out of the window as they drove up Copenhagen Street and overhearing the adults talking in hushed tones about how rough things were round there. There were rows and rows of tenement houses, all boarded up with 'LEB OFF' written in paint on each one. It was years before Margaret realized that LEB OFF wasn't some terrible swear word but stood for London Electricity Board, who had switched off the supply to the blocks.

Margaret has friends who came down from Lossiemouth

in Scotland in the 1950s and lived in big old houses where each family had one room, the women sleeping together, three or four to a bed, different families sharing cooking facilities on the landing. You can see why the properties were condemned and people desperate to escape poverty got involved in crime.

There were certain big families in Islington that people still talk about. Some very tasty individuals who made crime their business. The famous HMP Pentonville was the local nick so it was easy to keep in touch if one of your family was banged up.

One of the local social workers was a woman from a posh family of Edinburgh doctors. She'd been to Oxford University but treated her job as a vocation. I don't think I ever met her but they said she was a bit eccentric. She didn't get her shoes mended and she cut her own hair and always seemed to have a house full of families she was looking after. Young single mums in real trouble, sometimes. She would find ways of getting them a fridge or a bed. If there was someone on the edge she'd manage to get them the help they needed from the NHS. The good social workers tried their best, though it must have seemed a bit overwhelming. A lot of the time, neighbours would help out in a crisis.

As messed up as I was, I always felt I benefitted from the best in the community, thanks mainly to families who took me in and the poor teachers who had to put up with me. I needed help to find my way and, thankfully, someone was always there at the right moment.

15

A Big Chance

IN 1985, A FEW WEEKS AFTER MY THIRTEENTH BIRTHDAY, something happened to get me out of the hole I was in.

At drama group, there was a lovely woman called Sandra who helped out with all the contract stuff when we got roles and she took me under her wing a bit. She liked my acting and knew things were pretty messed up for me in the outside world. Not that I'd told anyone there what things were really like at home but I think they must have guessed. Whenever I was offered roles, they had to get permission from my aunt, as my main foster parent and legal guardian, so it wasn't hard to work out that I wasn't from a regular family home with a loving mum and dad.

Sandra was of Jamaican extraction and had a lovely rich voice and a huge laugh. She sometimes brought in jerk chicken and let me taste it. I can still remember the specific tangy, spicy flavour. Sandra made her own jerk sauce and marinated the meat in the fridge for maximum strength. I craved a mother figure who gave me encouragement, so I always looked forward to seeing her.

Alongside Sandra, there was another great woman, Wendy Fletcher, who acted as the agent for those of us who got picked for roles. Her son Dexter was also in my drama school. Dexter was six years older than me but let me knock about with him. He became a bit like an older brother, though he was totally different to my real brothers. Dexter was already doing well and since those days, he has had a long and successful career as an actor and director.

Mick was always on at me, saying, 'You can't act,' which knocked my confidence. It gnawed away that he might be right. But Sandra and Wendy helped me to believe that maybe I did have some ability.

If it wasn't for Dexter, Wendy, Sandra and, of course, Anna Scher, I'm pretty sure I would have stopped turning up for class around that time. I was feeling increasingly trapped in my day-to-day reality. The part-time classes at drama school and the small roles I got just weren't enough for me to escape it. I was still in the same place, with the same reputation, mixing with the same people. I admit I got a buzz out of thieving. I loved it and I guess I was addicted to it. Away from Anna Scher's, my reputation among everybody who knew me was a little guy who fought, thieved and gambled. Days away from the reality of my life here and there weren't going to break any bad habits. Once I was back on the streets I was sucked straight back into the same destructive cycle. I didn't see how anyone from my background could have any legitimate success. In the world I came from, the only people who were successful were thieves and gangsters. I knew unless something radically changed then I was going to go down the route of being a criminal, that things would get worse and worse.

I really, really wanted to be in the BBC children's drama, *Grange Hill*. It was first broadcast in 1978 and from when I was eleven or twelve years old that programme represented the pinnacle of being a young actor for me. I just loved the fact it was a drama about school. It hit on a lot of good subjects. Every week I'd rush back to watch it. It had a great theme tune as well and it was a really big show. Everyone at school watched *Grange Hill* and talked about it. The storylines dealt with stuff kids could really identify with, all kinds of important issues. I bought into every character, even though a lot of people from my drama school were in *Grange Hill* so in real life they were my mates. At one point, a kid I was best friends with, John Shannon, even had one of the main parts, playing Robbie Wright. Still, I was completely hooked.

It wasn't just the acting side that appealed, it was knowing that if I was in the show I wouldn't be going to school. At one point, I think ten or twenty mates from my drama school were in *Grange Hill*. I was jealously watching them, thinking why am I not in it? All the kids wanted it. You knew that a part in *Grange Hill* could be long term, a four-year job, perhaps, as your character moved up through the school years. I'd never have had to go to real school, although I'd have had tutoring.

I did have an audition but I didn't get the part. I was gutted. The funny thing was, in hindsight, if I'd got into *Grange Hill* and become well known for that, I probably wouldn't have got the role of Ricky in *EastEnders*, so I've no regrets. A lot of the kids in *Grange Hill* became well known, then struggled to get anything else because of that one high-profile role. They were typecast. The casting people were going, 'Sorry, he's done *Grange Hill*.' So for some child actors, the transition to adult roles was really difficult. Others successfully moved on, like Susan Tully and Todd Carty, who were both in *Grange Hill* and, later, *EastEnders*. Todd had played Tucker Jenkins as a kid. All the boys at school wanted to be Tucker.

The kids that were in *Grange Hill* were famous. Walking down the street they'd get recognized and shouted at. I'd had a taste of fame after doing the improvised 'No Adults Allowed' on *TV-am*. It got me recognized – 'Oh, there's that kid off the TV' – but *Grange Hill* was a bigger thing, always in my face. I knew almost everyone in it and felt like it was my destiny to be in the series too but it just wasn't to be.

Then an opportunity came up for a part in an epic, big-budget film, *Revolution*. Though I almost didn't go to the first audition, my confidence was so low. Sandra and Wendy persuaded me to try but I didn't bother telling Carol and Mick about it, feeling sure I wouldn't be offered anything anyway.

The audition started in the usual way with the casting people coming in to watch the class, then picking someone they liked. I still remember it clearly. The technique they often used with the kids at Anna Scher's was to give us what they called a 'feed line', getting us to make something up from there and see where it took us. It might be something like, 'Where's my pencil case?' Then you'd go up to another kid and start a conversation, or more often an argument, and it would develop from that. It was mostly arguments. Screaming and shouting.

At the audition for *Revolution* the feed line was, 'I have to tell you your mum's died,' so the reaction they wanted was lots of emotion. Of course, that line brought it all back for me, how it was losing my mum all those years before, and I felt it for real. That was what probably got me the job, because I did a bloody good job of crying.

I was called back for two follow-up auditions. The last one was at the Hyde Park Hotel, which is now the Mandarin Oriental, a very swish establishment in central London. Everywhere I looked were chandeliers, antiques in cabinets, paintings and lots of marble. Staff in fancy uniforms. It was unbelievably swanky. I felt as if I was walking into

Buckingham Palace. I saw Dexter there and I thought they'd want to give him the part. Then someone told me they wanted to match us up to see if we could look similar enough for me to play a younger version of him. Dexter had big lips, so I stood there pouting, trying to make mine look like his.

I remember being called back and walking into the room, still doing my best to pout. They took one look at my contortions and someone said, 'Are you OK?'

I asked if I'd done alright and they told me, 'Oh yeah, you've got the job – now come up and meet Al Pacino.' I was too young to have seen any Pacino films, all I knew was that he was a famous American actor, a big movie star. I thought I was going to meet Rocky – Sylvester Stallone. The producers thought this was hilarious but it turned out that one of them, Irwin Winkler, had produced all the Rocky films so I got given the latest Rocky T-shirt before it hit the shops. Which saved me from nicking one.

I was cast as Ned, the son of Al Pacino's character, Tom Dobb. I found out later that Dexter had indeed been cast as the older Ned but that my role would be the bigger part and was a pivotal role in the film.

I still believe that my first audition, reacting to the line about my mum dying, got me the part. In many ways, because acting was a release for me, throwing myself into emotional situations would feel very real – and most thirteen-year-olds don't have so much to draw on as I did. Acting is about letting yourself go and losing yourself in your character's situation, which I found easy to do. I hope I have a capacity to move people when I act. I think that's partly what made Ricky so successful as a character, because he could make people laugh and cry. What was always drummed into us by our drama teachers was believability. Whatever you say or do, people have to believe it. So when I started to properly learn scripts, I knew I had to memorize them and then almost forget they were lines so when it came to the performance I could make them sound like I was saying them for the first time. It was a normal and natural thing for me to do.

Word soon got round I'd landed a part in a big movie and everyone was over the moon. This was on another level to the acting jobs I'd had before. My brothers were pleased and proud of me, so were the Wooders. Aunt Carol and Mick were excited too. It felt good to be getting something right, as if the time I spent at Anna Scher's school was at last coming to something. At times, though, it seemed everyone else was more excited about *Revolution* than I was. But then it dawned on me what a big deal it was and the nerves kicked in. I was the one who had to do the job, which felt like a huge pressure. The more the people around me became seriously over-excited, the more nervous and pressured I began to feel. I went through all kinds of emotions.

My film role became the talk of the town, so to speak. 'Local Boy to Star in Movie with Al Pacino.' There wasn't a single person in Islington who hadn't heard about it, or at least that's how it seemed to me. People came up to me in the street wanting to know about it, asking questions about Al Pacino. I tried to deal with the fuss by telling myself it was just a job.

On the morning I left to start on *Revolution*, I was packed and ready to go long before the car came to pick me up. I got into the back seat and was whisked away to another world, knowing it would be a while before I came home.

Revolution was about the American War of Independence, the struggle to break from the British Crown and establish the United States of America. The conflict, from 1775 to 1783, is possibly one of the most important parts of American history. We didn't film in America, though, our locations were mostly in the UK – King's Lynn, Dartmoor and Plymouth. We shot some scenes in Norway. The production was on a massive scale.

Early on we shot some night scenes on Dartmoor. That wasn't easy. Because it was protected land we had to park the vehicles some distance away then walk about a mile and a half to get to the location. The mud was up to our knees. And this was before we'd even started a long night shoot. It felt like we were there every single night in March and it was below freezing with sleet and zero cover, just out there in the elements.

It was an enormously ambitious thing for them to do. The budget kept creeping up and up because they were having to replicate another period in another country and it was really tough to make it authentic. The battle scenes had to be realistic, with us covered in mud and freezing our arses off all night.

Because this was the 1980s, before special effects could generate realistic crowds, there were what seemed to me like thousands and thousands of extras in the battle scenes, and little tipis covering the whole hillside. No wonder the film cost so much!

The extras in their moccasins were getting frostbite. It was a physically tough film for everybody. The cold – I've never been so cold in my life and I hope I never will be again. And it might seem like a small thing compared to the night shoots but another thing that bugged me was the quality of my costume – it was incredibly itchy. It doesn't sound like much, just a silly thing, but for someone like me who was used to wearing jeans and a T-shirt, suddenly I was in a raggedy period costume. It made me irritable, I have to admit. On hot days too, wearing rough sacking around my neck, and itchy shirts and trousers, was horrible.

I had to get dirtier and dirtier as the film progressed, so if you watch it and see me getting more and more scruffy, that was authentic. I had the same pair of trousers throughout the whole film. The costumes did look brilliant even though they were difficult to wear.

In spite of all of the freezing weather, sleepless nights and itchy clothes, we somehow got the job done.

Drama lessons don't come much better than working with Al Pacino. By then, he was known for films like *The Godfather*, *Serpico* and *Scarface*, and had picked up several Oscar nominations. When I started on *Revolution*, there was a lot for us to work through together to make our father and son relationship convincing, so we quickly got into a routine where every day I'd go to his trailer and we'd run lines, whatever we were doing that day. He had a way about him that meant when we sat down something would click into place and we became the characters we were playing. I got totally into it. On set, the scenes just flowed effortlessly from the work we'd put in together beforehand. It was almost like the cameras and crew weren't there.

As a method actor, Pacino's technique was to go deep into his character. As he was playing my father he formed a strong connection with me. There was give and take on both sides but he was my mentor and took a personal interest in a way he didn't for any of the other kids on set. The stronger our bond, the better his performance. I was conscious that if I was good at my part, it would be good for him and also that if I failed to come up with the goods it would be bad for all my fellow cast members. If I was distracted or was fucking around, he'd let me know he disapproved. But I was able to switch it on when I needed to. I think that comes naturally as a kid. Though I found the same thing as an adult when I was in *EastEnders*, too. I'd have a big scene coming up and I'd be joking around but as soon as the camera rolls you switch it on and give your all.

It was amazing to be so young and working so closely with one of the greatest actors of all time. Working with Pacino gave me some of my biggest acting lessons ever – seeing how he used the method technique to get into character, how professional he was when the cameras started to roll and how much of himself he brought to his parts.

At the end of the day, he must have seen some talent in me to invest so much time in me. It wasn't just the odd rehearsal or performance here and there – it was constant, intensive. So we built a relationship and he brought out a side of me that made me a better actor. I tried not to be overwhelmed – and for the most part, I wasn't. It turns out that when you see Al Pacino day in, day out, you sometimes forget that he's an absolute legend. Though I couldn't ever really forget – it was Al Pacino, after all, and I was thirteen years old and playing his son in my first big role!

In between takes, sometimes I didn't know what to do with myself. There was a lot of hanging about waiting, then intense bursts of pressure where I had to try and get everything right, so I was full of adrenaline. The devil finds work for idle hands and a hyper teenager with an overload of adrenaline is a dangerous cocktail. Sometimes I just couldn't calm down.

Our hotel was lovely, far removed from the chaotic atmosphere I'd grown up in, but instead of enjoying it I somehow couldn't escape the chaos in my head. I remember sitting in the plush dining room carving my

name on the table with a knife I'd found. My dysfunc-
tional background was coming out more and more, and
my attitude got worse. If I was in trouble, it was never
the director, Hugh Hudson, who told me off. There was
a pecking order of people from the production who dealt
with me before I'd be put in front of Hugh. Generally,
they were nice people but if I got too out of hand, they
made sure I knew about it.

One morning after I'd been told off yet again, I stayed
out of the way, hiding round the back of the trailer
smoking a cigarette from a pack of fags I'd nicked. Al
Pacino saw me later and asked me to come and have a
chat with him. He said, 'Why didn't you come and see
me today?' He had a bit of a go at me for not running
lines with him like we were supposed to. He was being
strict about it and I apologized. I felt ashamed because
by then I looked up to him a lot – in a way, he seemed
to understand me. He knew I had no parents and was
from a difficult background, even though we didn't really
talk about it. When we weren't running lines we usually
just cracked little jokes and stuff, and got along really
well. But he got very serious that day and told me,
'You've got to behave a bit better.' After that, he sort of
took me under his wing like a real father figure, not just
when we were playing our roles. He didn't have kids of
his own then and I found out later he had considered
adopting me. One time he said, 'Come out to New York
when this is finished.' We kept in touch and years later

I took my first serious girlfriend, Amanda, to New York, and he invited us to stay with him and his partner at the time, Diane Keaton. We still catch up every now and then.

I was fortunate to work with some incredible actors on *Revolution*, including Donald Sutherland, who played a brutal British solider. Donald was a big man with a big presence and properly scary when he was in character. Like Pacino, he kept his character going between takes but as soon as we finished he would totally transform into a really funny guy. He made me laugh a lot. I think he liked me, though he and I didn't have the same bond I had with Al Pacino or with the female lead, Nastassja Kinski. Donald Sutherland remains one of the people I've acted with that I have great respect for. His son, Kiefer, would come on set sometimes. This was before his big break in *The Lost Boys*, a brilliant film. There's a great picture of me with Donald in costume at the end of a scene, acting daft.

There was a scene where my character, young Ned, was captured by Donald Sutherland's character and whipped to within an inch of his life. We filmed it during a night shoot when it was pissing down with rain and freezing cold. We'd rehearsed and improvised the bones of the scene because they knew I was good at improvising. I'd been made to learn about ten pages of script and notes from the director, then we were given time to rehearse and improvise around it. When the scene was done, there was a real buzz about how good it was and talk of me being shortlisted for a Best Supporting Actor Oscar. Unfortunately, once the film was released, any talk of Oscar nominations went away.

16

Revolution

A LOT HAPPENED ON THE SET OF *REVOLUTION*. I DEVELOPED my first massive teenage crush and became seriously infatuated with the actress Nastassja Kinski. I'd never met anyone like her. It felt as if she came from another planet, one that was light years away from Chapel Market. She oozed star quality and would glide into a room, smile her beautiful smile, then come up and speak to me in this sexy German accent. She even smelled amazing. I became completely besotted. She was twenty-four, married and had a little kid with the Egyptian film producer Ibrahim Moussa, who was about forty and lived abroad. I can't remember how much of this I knew at the time but whatever I'd heard, I did a damn good job of ignoring. The fact she had a husband and a child didn't put me off one little bit.

At one point, she disappeared when she was supposed to be on set and no one could find her or knew where she'd gone. It turned out she was in Paris having her hair cut – she couldn't find a good enough hairdresser in King's Lynn, apparently. Stuff like that made me realize I was indeed a world away from Islington.

Nastassja used to spoil me, buy me presents and give me little cuddles. Al Pacino bought me presents, too. He got me an Atari console with loads of games, which was all the rage back then. I think the hope was it would calm me down a bit and it sort of worked, sometimes. Remember that, aside from the problems in my background, I was also the youngest actor with a main part, so it was strange for me, living in a grown-up world.

Whenever we went to film at other locations, the big stars like Al Pacino, Donald Sutherland and Nastassja Kinski were given houses to stay in. Al Pacino would invite me to stay at whatever house he'd been given, but so would Nastassja. The more time I spent with her the more infatuated I became. I loved everything about her. I felt her incredible star quality. I could understand why people hired her and why every man she met seemed to melt in her presence. Even Al Pacino. She was just being kind to a scruffy kid but I was thinking, I'm a teenager. I've hit puberty. I'm wanking and everything. Give it a year or two – maybe I'll be in with a chance!

Hugh Hudson had directed *Chariots of Fire*, which

scooped a heap of awards in 1982, including the Best Picture Oscar, so it was no surprise that the set of *Revolution* was littered with talent, including Richard O'Brien and Robbie Coltrane. Annie Lennox played a prostitute called the Liberty Woman, with wild red hair that flowed all down her back. She was lovely.

The atmosphere on set wasn't always easy going. There was a scene where Al refused to carry on because he was having an argument with Hugh. Hugh wanted a certain thing to be one way and Al wanted it to be another. Filming stopped for it to get sorted out and the producer, Irwin Winkler, had to step in.

The young actors on the film had their own tutors and chaperones. There were forty kids, including a few from Anna Scher's, coming over from London. Only the kids who came from America had their parents on set. The rest of us were on our own, except for our chaperones.

The fact that the job, from pre-production to filming and post-production, lasted almost a whole year was a lot to get my head around. A year feels like forever when you're thirteen – remember how long just six weeks of school holidays used to feel. It meant I was pretty much out of school entirely, which was OK with me. I was only too happy to leave Highbury Grove behind, get away from all the fighting. I was up for a change. It was like a complete transition for me.

During filming, Sharon Harris was my tutor and she was also in charge of recruiting the other tutors and chaperones. She recruited Sallyann Sexton to be the main chaperone and personally responsible for me. Sallyann had been teaching drama and was used to working with kids. I was her main responsibility but she ended up looking after a bunch of kids from time to time, too.

The tutors and chaperones were hired before we were even cast. Sharon was responsible for dealing with licenses, sorting out our education, all the paperwork, everything. Lots of agents – quite rightly so – want to know what they're dealing with when a child goes onto a film set. The director would know, acting-wise, what a kid was about but it was other people who knew what the real child, as opposed to the actor, was going to be like. I think when I was cast there was a question as to who would be the right person to be my mentor, to be with me 24/7, and guide me through this film set, this adventure, working with movie stars. Being away from home and having a certain freedom, living in hotel rooms, working with other children I'd never ever met before – younger and older – was a tall order. It was a big growing-up time for me.

I remember my very first meeting with Sallyann. Although she met so many kids, she says I had a particularly cheeky face and she immediately fell for me. I have the best memories of working with her and Sharon. They had to be strict, they had to be fun and they had to be kind. You couldn't rule me, I was a maverick, that was the thing. I would do what I wanted. Sallyann was there to steer me in the right direction, down the right road.

I do think a lot of credit for the success of my performance in *Revolution* was down to Sallyann. She was the one person who was there with me 24/7, through the good and the bad, all the new experiences, attempting to impose some discipline, just like a parent would, but also to be on that incredible journey with me. I was doing full filming days and children's work laws were very strict. We were permitted to do a nine-hour working day. Within those nine hours, we had to have three hours' education. That was where Sharon came in. She would organize the whole day's schedule. She had tutors coming in for different subjects, liaising with schools and sorting out breaks. It was tough going for them. Every child was cast because they were 'characters' and were therefore never easy to wrangle into getting school-work done. Sharon would try and get me to sit down and work but I didn't really do that much. She was always kind and said, 'I think Sid did what he could to the best of his ability.' Getting me to sit down at all was an amazing feat!

Sharon was 'the circus master' – that was how she described herself. To try to control, never mind teach, me and forty other kids was a difficult thing to do. She had to keep everything within the regulations. That was her responsibility. You'd have people from the local authority come down to check everything was being done by the book. If they found anything wrong, they could shut down the whole film. So it was a very serious set up.

Sharon described me as 'spirited' but that was a huge understatement. I would push boundaries. They said I was unorthodox, that you never quite knew what would come out of my mouth. Neither did I! Luckily for me, my character exactly suited the role.

I was a bit of a Marmite person back then. People would either love hanging out with me or be driven crazy. I was good company but Sharon also called me 'a little scallywag boy'. Luckily, she had brothers and she knew just how to deal with a boy who wanted to kick a ball instead of doing his maths homework.

There was a lot to juggle between my education and my role in the film. The tutors couldn't come down with too hard a rod. We might be supposed to be doing maths but if Sharon knew in half an hour I'd be on set recalling sad memories, having to sob and cry in Al Pacino's arms – real sensitive scenes with big close-ups – it was vital to make the situation conducive so that I would feel comfortable. Although the state of my maths was enough to make anyone cry.

I knew that Sharon and Sallyann would look after me, care for me and try and get me into the right zone mentally so I felt ready to do what I needed to. They were very protective of me and made sure I wasn't being over-worked. They knew I was a free spirit and let me do what I wanted but they also created a safe environment for me.

They really had their work cut out, though. Filming schedules changed all the time and you had to be there on standby in case you were needed. Sometimes Sharon would be supervising forty children through their lessons at nine in the morning and then there'd be no filming for you that day so you had to do other things. You still had to stay on set though, and it was over to our chaperones and tutors to kill time with us. We'd all be saying, 'Can we go back, can we go to the hotel?' We wanted to escape and chill out. On set we were in trailers and portacabins in what was basically a car park. There were double-decker catering buses, big tents where you'd go and get your food. It was OK when it was good weather but when the rain came the chaperones had to work extra hard to look after us.

Back then there were no PlayStations, no mobile phones, nothing to entertain us like you might have nowadays. I had my Atari but that was back at the hotel. The chaperones and tutors were imaginative though and we created daytime activities. We did quizzes and things like that, and then us kids would sit down with members of the crew who weren't working and they'd tell us a bit about their jobs. Carpenters would tell us about their skills or someone from the lighting crew or wardrobe and the hair and make-up stylists would talk to us. You got to hear a whole wide range of people's experiences. It was a good thing because we had a lot of hours to kill on set. In a way, it was hard *not* to be a handful.

I was considered a bit too much sometimes. Once we were walking down King's Lynn High Road, where everyone was busy doing their shopping. We had been told to remain anonymous. My brain interpreted that instruction as meaning the exact opposite. I cranked up Barrington Levy's 'Here I Come' on my ghettoblaster and sang along to the lyrics, some of which went, 'Here I come! Whoah!', which

I'm sure the people of King's Lynn appreciated. Sallyann asked me to be more discreet but I was having too good a time so I just got louder. I'm pretty sure some of the locals gave me a nod and a smile and shimmied their hips a little.

Sharon and Sallyann knew that, deep down, I responded to warmth and kindness. They knew I had lost my mum and that things at home were not great, so they were aware I was looking for love and to be part of a family. Sallyann still says that coming from a background like mine makes you grow up faster but, at the same time, when your childhood is cut short you're always a bit of a child. The older I've got the more I've realized that's true and that there's a damaged child inside of me that I've been trying to heal. At times doing well, and others not so well.

Back then, Sallyann was only twenty-one, so still young herself, with a three-year-old son, Taylor. He was a lovely little boy. To come to work on *Revolution* she had to leave him temporarily. I think a lot of the love she had for her son was displaced to me because I gave her somewhere to put that motherly instinct. She tells me now I had a 'stardust' thing. She didn't tell me that at the time! Probably just as well as it would have given me a big head to match my big mouth.

I don't think any family ever visited me the whole time I was making *Revolution*, particularly because parents and guardians weren't allowed. Sallyann says now that made her feel even more protective. I didn't expect anything else.

I was glad to be away from my Aunt Carol and her partner. I didn't miss home at all. I never felt lonely or unhappy.

Though I was close to being sacked a couple of times. Some people didn't know how to handle me and that seemed like the answer. I think I would have been blissfully unaware of this at the time. I would have thought it was funny to push the boundaries.

I used to escape from the set, go into the town and run riot. One time, I bought a load of those noisy fake guns you used to get – all banned these days – that had paper rolls of ammunition filled with tiny pellets of real gunpowder. You'd get a great smell of the gunpowder when you fired and a satisfyingly big bang. I also bought a load of sweets, crazy colours and exploding flavours, filled with additives that are no doubt also banned these days, as too many would turn even the most sedate child into a hyperactive nightmare. I handed out the sweets to any other kid I could find in the hotel we were staying at and we ran around on a sugar and chemical rush, causing total chaos, playing gangsters and screaming our heads off. The staff went mental and complained to the producers.

In the end, what Sallyann and Sharon did for me ran so much deeper than just keeping me in check. They became like family to me. On a film set you can really bond with people – it's a special environment, so far from the everyday, and when you're all thrown together like that you get to know each other really well. For all the craziness of being on a set you do eventually get into routines and it does feel like being part of a functioning family.

I was at an impressionable age and what Sallyann and Sharon – and even Al Pacino and Nastassja Kinski – represented were grown-ups who looked out for me and shaped who I became. That's all anyone can ask for, really – especially someone like me. I was lucky to have them.

17

New Horizons

FOR THE PEOPLE OF KING'S LYNN, IT MUST HAVE FELT like the circus had come to town when *Revolution* arrived. Norfolk might seem an unlikely setting for the American Revolution but Hugh Hudson had scouted various locations and decided it was perfect. The only other contender was Williamsburg, in the US, which Hugh thought was too much like a museum piece. King's Lynn has an old dock area that was just what he was looking for. It stood in for a battle location – don't ask me which battle – but it was meant to double for New York, the harbour of the Hudson river. Nearby was Hunstanton and all those parts of Norfolk that are very flat, so they did one of the battles there. There were a lot of battles.

The main streets of King's Lynn are full of old merchants'

houses and historic buildings. They are cobbled and very pretty and exactly the kind of place you'd want if you were trying to replicate the late eighteenth century. Nowadays you could use computer-generated imagery, or CGI, to create the right period, down to the cobblestones, but we had none of that so they took great care to make the set look right and used facades to make the buildings fit the period. We shot a scene – me and Al Pacino, with a huge number of extras – right outside Customs House. My character, Ned, had signed up to the army and was separated from his furious father, played by Al. It was a really affecting scene.

Everything was real on set – every fire, every candle, down to the smallest detail to make the whole thing credible. You can imagine the hours the crew put in. I bet the people of King's Lynn couldn't believe what was happening to their quiet little town. We used hundreds of locals as extras, playing sailors, soldiers, pirates, all kinds.

At night, I'd get to go 'home' to the hotel, right on the square. I loved that. In the mornings we'd leave the hotel – it was like trying to herd snakes with us kids – walk through town, through the shopping precinct and down to the shoot's unit base, where the classrooms were, as well as hair and make-up, costume trailers, lighting rigs, all of that. Further down towards the harbour, the feel of the place became quite Dickensian. TV versions of *David Copperfield* and *Martin Chuzzlewit* have since been filmed in King's Lynn, too.

After King's Lynn, we filmed in Plymouth, where we

shot more of the shipyard scenes. This was when the Native American contingent of actors turned up. Things got a lot more exciting when they were around. When they came into the hotel for the first time, it was a sensational moment. I was sitting in reception, probably with nothing to do at that point and looking for a distraction, and in they walked with Stetsons and saddles and my jaw just dropped to the floor. That was a distraction, all right. It was already a big movie but when they came in they upped the ante and it really felt like I was somewhere different. Everything took a little lift when they appeared with their horses; it all felt more showbiz and even more amazing.

Skeeter Vaughan, whose Cherokee name was Grey Otter, played the old chief. He'd acted with John Wayne and appeared in the TV series *The Six Million Dollar Man*. He was a professional stuntman and knife-thrower, a mix of showman and warrior, and seeing him blew my mind.

One great thing about getting a role in something like *Revolution* when you're young is you meet people from all over the world and your horizons expand. They'd already broadened a fair bit back in Chapel Market but this was a whole new deal.

Not all of the film's Native American roles were played by the likes of Skeeter. I guess that's just the way it was in those days. Sallyann's son was mixed race and they used to scan the script to see if there was any small part he could possibly play, so that she could have him with her on set for a couple of weeks. They did find something for him, a Native American character, which wouldn't happen now as we give more respect to people's backgrounds and cast accordingly.

One of my favourite moments was on the way to Plymouth when Sharon took Al Pacino to WHSmith. Lots of the cast and crew took the train and Sharon thought Al might want something to read on the journey. He chose some magazines and sauntered up to the till to pay for them. The poor young Saturday boy's jaw practically hit the floor. He was staring at him and couldn't quite believe what he was seeing – a movie star in the shop. Eventually, he managed to squeak some words out: 'Are you who I think you are or do you just look like him?'

Al said, 'Yeah, I probably am the person you think I am.' By then, the whole queue had noticed. It's not often you get Al Pacino buying magazines in WHSmith, so fair play to the boy for plucking up the courage to ask.

One of the hardest challenges was when we shot a big death scene at Shepperton. That was a week of being on set all day, every day. It was tough. They wanted me to do a lot of improvising, so we'd rehearse over and over again. It was a lot for a kid. You have to make those feelings real somehow and then keep doing it again and again. Maybe one thing that helped was that *Revolution* felt crazy and chaotic – but so did the life I already knew, although obviously in a very different way. I was a child; I was adaptable and craziness and chaos seemed normal to me.

I reckon that's why it didn't throw me that much and I was able to do my job.

The most exotic location we filmed in was Norway and that was because we had some Norwegian investment in the film. We went there by private jet in the summer of 1985. It was just cast and a small crew for those scenes – what's called a 'reduced unit'. Al Pacino was there and he had a *Playboy* magazine with him – that was back when *Playboy* was considered sophisticated, with essays and politics and stuff. The adults were offered champagne and everyone other than Al got slaughtered. I tried to grab a cheeky drink but Al was like, 'No, no, he's not having one,' so that was that. I know now that he had struggled with alcohol from a young age and had been sober since the late seventies, so was looking out for me because of his own experiences.

For some reason, that flight out there sticks in my mind as the epitome of showbiz. Leaving everyone else behind and whizzing off on a private jet. It was obviously my first time on a private jet and, to be honest, I didn't even realize that was what it was at first! Dexter Fletcher was there, too, because this was around the time in the story when Dexter would begin playing the older version of me.

When our plane landed, we were in the bloody Arctic Circle. It was fabulous. The Norwegian production company greeted us and welcomed us to Stavanger. We were given funny flowers. One of the first things that happened was we had an emergency meeting, which everyone was forced to attend. What was it about? How expensive the booze was! They said it cost a fortune to drink there and you needed to be careful. Two pints down and you'd basically drunk your life savings away.

We left rocky Stavanger and took a helicopter even further into the Arctic Circle. Everyone was singing the theme tune from the TV show *M.A.S.H.*, which had helicopters in the opening titles.

We started to film a hundred or so yards from where we had landed. It was amazing, like being on the moon, hilly and bleak, with streams cascading down and blinding sunlight. To shoot the scenes, we had to get right to the top of the fjord and then the cameras were set up over on the other side of the ravine. Because we were in the Arctic Circle, we were in the land of the midnight sun. That meant the sun never set, even if it was midnight or two o'clock in the morning. We would wrap after a shoot and then get back to where we were staying and it was still light, no matter what time it was.

Up until then, on set there were probably around two hundred or so members of crew because there was so much going on. When we got to Norway, the scenes were much simpler as a lot of the action was shot from a distance. There were no extras, just the main cast. This meant it was intense in a whole different way to how it had been in our other locations.

It was a brilliant place to shoot. For some of the scenes we had to be up at the top of springs, right at the top of the fjord, and when we got there on the day of filming, all the wildflowers had popped open. They literally had to pick all the flowers before we could start shooting, for the sake of continuity. So we had teams of people picking a whole hillside of flowers. We could work round the clock, though, because of the constant daylight.

I have to admit that at some points, like at midnight, I'd think, fucking hell I should be asleep in bed by now. But because it was broad daylight you couldn't quite believe it was night. The other thing that made it harder to sleep was that I had teenage girls trying to get into my bedroom. Sallyann had to chase them off. She'd tell them to go away and they'd sneak back and try to climb in through my bedroom window. They were about sixteen, and Sallyann was shocked because I was only thirteen at that point.

Honestly, I think they were looking for Al Pacino. His Norwegian groupies. It'd be nice to claim that I had fans in Norway even before *Revolution* came out but it's a safer bet to say they were on the hunt for Al. It didn't matter to me, though, I found it unbelievably exciting. I couldn't get my head round it. It felt like one minute I was at the Wooders' in Islington, the next I was in a hotel in another country being treated like a movie star.

When filming ended, I had to say goodbye to Al Pacino, Nastassja Kinski, Donald Sutherland and all the other cast and crew, who had become my world during the past year. I loved Nastassja's kindness and her cuddles, and Al treating me like a real son. It was so tough, realizing it was all over, but I knew the experience had changed me. In a way, you could say it had saved me. I'd been out of my surroundings long enough to feel like there was an alternative.

I think when the film wrapped it was a huge thing for all of us. I hate to use the 'journey' word but that was what we'd been on together. I'd also experienced a sense of being loved. I'd worked hard and knew I was good at my job. I was finally being treated in a way I'd not been before. Sallyann even wanted to adopt me. I came back home with her after the film but she felt she had to let me go as she didn't want to overstep the mark with Aunt Carol and Mick. She said she missed me and worried about me for years afterwards. We're still friends after all this time – proof the bond between us was real.

With the shoot over, we were done with the glamorous helicopters and fans, and into post-edit. I have to admit I found the post-edit pretty frustrating. You had to sit in a small cinema and you'd watch bits of the movie without any dialogue. A small line would go across the screen from left to right. As soon as it hit the end, that was your exact cue to speak. It was quite difficult doing this, and there was a lot of it to do. Maybe something had gone wrong with the sound, or it had not been checked during the shoot, so all these bits of dialogue couldn't be heard clearly enough and had to be dubbed over. I did some voices other than my own because I was quite good at that.

I think Al Pacino was frustrated with the process, too. He would be doing his lines and in between would let out these huge pissed-off sighs. The poor guys working with him were just projectionists and a sound guy, I don't think the director was there. Sallyann was, though, and she remembers a moment where the poor technical guy was asking Al to go again one more time, and then again, and Al was getting more and more wound up. Eventually he said, 'What's the problem?' The tech guy explained they needed just a little more clarity and Al told him, 'You can either have clarity or you can have performance.' That right there is a classic Al Pacino line.

I did what I had to do in post-production. It had been a long process by then but I had got used to it. I had the right attitude, at last. I was a professional and I was surrounded by great professionals, so I wanted to give as much as I could.

You hear a lot about huge films from the seventies and eighties. I don't know if they really make them like that anymore or if they can even afford to. Huge sets, endless extras and locations, and incredibly long shooting times. *Revolution* was one of those. It became its own little world within a world and everyone working on it probably created their own little world within that too. It was mad and wonderful but also gruelling, and you had to find your own way of surviving so that you could get through it.

The sad thing was that the production company, Goldcrest, made the director rush out the film for the Christmas market before it was finished. Apparently, Hugh Hudson wanted to add narration but there wasn't time. The film felt too long and confusing and on release it was a huge flop. *Time* magazine called it, 'An almost inconceivable disaster.' No chance of Oscar nominations, then. It was such a shame.

When it started to dawn on me that the one thing that had made me feel happy since losing Mum had gone wrong, it messed me up a bit, especially after such a massive build up. I tried to avoid thinking about it for as long as possible. Move on, I thought. Move onto the next thing. The bad reviews didn't filter through to me for a while. When it properly sank in, I was gutted. It gnawed away. I knew how much fucking effort everyone had made to pull it off. And after everything, it hadn't worked out.

I was also left thinking that if the film had been a smash hit, who knew where my career would have gone. I might have been signed up and straight off to Hollywood. As things were, work had gone a bit quiet. Even at that early age, I'd been in the business long enough to realize it wasn't the result that people hoped for. Other actors were leapfrogging me into bigger and better jobs.

The fact *Revolution* wasn't a smash wasn't because I'd done anything wrong but I still felt as if everything was tarnished. The comments about my own performance weren't bad. In fact, many people seemed to think I'd done a good job and that some of my scenes with Al Pacino were strong and deeply moving. But all of it, sadly, was overshadowed by the film doing so badly.

In some ways, I was aware that success could be more of a shock to the system than failure. Failure can be a kick in the teeth, especially when something is built up and then crashes down, but I was trained in hard knocks. I was used to them. They were almost my comfort zone. Deep down, the idea of success was scary to me.

Years later, Hugh Hudson finally wrote a voice-over, which Al Pacino recorded. *Revolution Revisited*, the director's cut, was released in 2012 as a BFI Blu-ray/DVD combo with an accompanying book (an honour only given to cinematic classics) and was dubbed a masterpiece by Philip French, one of the world's most respected film critics. He called it, 'Profound, poetic and original'. Hugh Hudson has called Al Pacino's performance 'some of the most moving acting he's ever done'.

Sadly, it will take a hell of a lot of Blu-ray sales, retrospective cinema screenings and online streaming to make up for the initial loss.

I've never sat down to watch the *Revisited* version. Most actors can't stand seeing themselves on screen and I'm exactly the same. The closest I got was when a friend was watching it and I glimpsed myself on screen. It was strange to see my younger self there – like seeing someone else. But I'm glad the film has been reappraised. Everyone involved put so much into it and it was good to finally see it get the credit it deserved, even after so long.

18

Back Down to Earth

AFTER *REVOLUTION*, I HAD TO GO BACK TO MY REAL life. And that wasn't easy.

While I was away filming, Aunt Carol, her partner, Mick and my brother Scott had left Stonefield Street and bought a house in Tottenham. I don't remember how I found out about us leaving Islington but I was gutted because the old flat had been my mum's and moving away felt like losing the last link to her. So it was hard to leave behind the old flat forever and it also separated me further from my older two brothers, Darren and Mark, who were still in Islington. Scott was such a mad Arsenal fan and he hated Tottenham Hotspur. So, from his point of view, of all the places to move to, Tottenham was the worst! He had strong ties to Islington, as all his friends were there, and he carried on going back there all the time.

On *Revolution*, we very occasionally had a couple of days off. I was mainly on call so I had to stay on set or nearby, even if I wasn't in a scene. When I was able to go home, I had a driver to take me, so the first time I saw the new place I was chauffeured there from the film set right to the front door. I remember looking out of the car window and thinking, 'Fuck, this looks well rough.'

The house was an ordinary two-up, two-down terrace. On my visits, I'd stay for a couple of days, then a car would come to pick me up again and take me back to the set. At that time, *Revolution* felt like my proper life and the house in Tottenham felt unreal. When I was there all I wanted was to get back to work.

But of course once *Revolution* was over, there was nowhere to escape to. There was no denying that the house in Tottenham *was* my real life.

Unsurprisingly, I landed back on earth with a bump. After an incredible year on *Revolution*, mixing with Al Pacino and Nastassja Kinski, it was a shock to suddenly find myself in Tottenham, which, back then, was rough and frightening. This was straight after the Broadwater Farm riot in 1985, which was sparked when a local Afro-Caribbean woman, Cynthia Jarrett, collapsed and died as police searched her home. Bricks were thrown, cars set on fire and a house close to ours burnt to the ground. PC Keith Blakelock was killed and one of his colleagues seriously injured. The week before, there had been riots in

Brixton when the police shot another black woman, Cherry Groce. Tensions were running high in London and elsewhere and, in October, things came to a head in Tottenham.

The estate was literally the top of our road. You could see the sprawl of Broadwater Farm from our house. I remember Scott and me getting mugged twice. They wanted to steal his jacket but he ended up giving them £20 instead. It was really scary. One time, on the underground, we had knives pulled on us – I think that was during the crack epidemic. My social life, and Scott's, was still in Islington. I'd get the 171 bus back to Tottenham and the long walk home from the bus stop, especially at night, was petrifying. I used to sprint it, to be honest.

I had the horrible feeling there was no way of escaping the past, that everything from my childhood, all the problems, were still there. After having had a taste of something better, nothing had really changed.

Not going out was sometimes the best bet. I'd always been into music, something I got from my mum and my brothers. On a Sunday at 5.30 p.m., I'd tune in for two hours to the official top 40 chart on Radio 1, recording my favourite hits onto my ghetto blaster. It was technically illegal but everybody did it, nobody got done for it and people still bought shitloads of music. Compilation albums, like *Now That's What I Call Music*, with all the hits, were popular. A new one seemed to come out every few months.

I was still into Madness, The Specials, plus Alexander O'Neal, George Benson. I loved reggae and thought Bob Marley and the Wailers were genius. Mark got me into

Motown and Stax. I was totally obsessed with Stevie Wonder. Still am. I've lost count of how many times I've seen him in concert around the world. I'd root around in second-hand record stores for stuff by underground artists. I knew they weren't rich and had a kind of honour code that I wouldn't nick stuff from these places.

I was big into my Walkman, which seemed groundbreaking in the eighties. To be able to put on headphones and listen to your favourite tunes on cassette wherever you were was exciting. The Walkman went everywhere with me. I always wanted to start my day with music and had a clock radio that was set to wake me up for school, so I'd get a blast of whatever happened to be playing on Radio 1. There were a few one-hit wonders, some crazy ones, I remember. More than once I got woken up by the fucking Birdie Song.

There was another big change on the horizon. I didn't want to go back to my old school, Highbury Grove. I was getting into too many fights there. I'd never liked fighting – I'd just been pushed into it from pretty much the moment I could walk. Also, when people found out I was acting, even the parts I'd got on TV shows before doing *Revolution*, I was bullied. After the movie I suspected it would be even worse.

Because I'd earned a bit of money, I was able to afford to switch to a private school, a decision I made with Carol and Mick. I knew that if I didn't take myself in a different direction, I'd slide back down again into a world of fighting and robbing. I made a vow to stop doing that. I think the film had given me a different perspective and I wanted something better for my life.

The new school was called Southbank, an international school near Victoria. It took about half an hour to walk from home to Turnpike Lane tube station, which seemed like a long way. And then it was about thirty minutes on the tube from there. I used to leave at a silly hour in the morning.

I was amazed when I first saw the new school. It was in a grand old house on Eccleston Square in Pimlico and was nothing like Highbury Grove. It was exciting for me because it wasn't what I had grown up with. The atmosphere was very relaxed and you could wear what you liked. Coming from a huge state school where everyone wore uniform and it was quite regimented, I was surprised how completely different it was. There were punk kids, piercings and tattoos on show and what seemed like every nationality – Iraqis, Iranians, Swedes – in my class.

I loved that. I loved the sense of the whole world being there.

It was mad, because we were allowed to smoke, kids lighting up in the canteen. Where I'd come from, if you got caught smoking, you would get battered. All of a sudden there are all these kids my age smoking and no one's in the least bit bothered.

The Southbank had a lovely atmosphere. For the first time in my life, I enjoyed going to school.

Studies-wise, I did alright. We were on a totally different

curriculum from what I was used to. And because there was no violence in the environment it meant I could focus on learning in a way I hadn't before. I was the class clown, though. I couldn't help it – I wanted to entertain everyone. It was in my blood by that point. I did routines that the kids loved but the teachers weren't so keen on. For me, though, I was getting to perform and I had an audience who lapped it up, so I kept on doing it. At the same time, I still wasn't great with discipline. I just wasn't used to having any.

One good thing about being class clown is that some people gravitate towards you and want to be friends because maybe they can see you're on similar wavelengths. One of the friends I made there, Karim, is still a mate now. That's not bad going at a school where some kids only stayed a term or so because so many were from the families of diplomats and always moving on.

Karim and a guy called Pazy were my main friends, both from the Middle East. They were proper good schoolmates. We had a right laugh and, meanwhile, I set about training them up in the ways of mischief.

Pazy used to live in Golders Green, which wasn't too far away from Tottenham, so I would go and stay over at his. We'd hang about outside the McDonalds and the station. It was a nice area, one that hasn't changed in decades. It's never been rough. Karim's family were in west London – kind of part of the Notting Hill set. They were both from wealthy families, proper rich kids. While I was still living in Tottenham, which was absolutely terrifying and considered by many people to be almost the worst

place in Britain. I would go from there to a posh private
school in the middle of Pimlico where my classmates were
rich kids. That was a pretty crazy contrast. But crazy
contrasts had become so much part of my life that it felt
pretty normal for me.

I was still spending time with Danny and in August 1986,
we went to see Queen at Wembley in what was probably
one of the greatest rock concerts of all time. I will never
forget it.

Queen were massive. Pretty much everyone had seen
them steal the show at Live Aid in 1985. I'd heard them
on the radio and seen them on *Top of the Pops* but I didn't
know that much about them so I'd not gone to the trouble
of nicking any of their albums. My brothers used to go to
concerts and Mark sold tickets for a tout, so could always
get some knock-off stuff. Darren and Scott loved their
music and never had to pay to get into a gig. That was
totally normal around our way.

Going to the Wembley gig was something I stumbled
into. Me and Danny got it into our heads that we wanted
to go to a concert – let's experience this, see what a big
concert is about. When we heard Queen were playing
Wembley on their *It's a Kind of Magic* tour we decided to
go and make a day of it. I don't think we told any adults
what we were up to.

Around that time, the Wooders had got a new contrap-
tion, a home sunbed on wheels that you could move from
room to room, plug in and lie there gently frying underneath

the UV lights. Sunbeds were quite the luxury, a new gimmick. The Wooders had a bit of money and liked all the latest fads. On the afternoon of the Queen gig, I thought, fuck it, I'll try the sunbed. Get myself nice and brown for the gig. I sneaked upstairs and switched it on, not realizing how powerful it was. I think I might have fallen asleep.

When I got up and looked in the mirror, my face was bright red, apart from the big white rings round my eyes where the goggles had been. So much for looking like Mr Cool Suntan Man at the concert. Then I had a brainwave. Sunglasses! If I wore shades and all the cool clobber, I'd go from looking like Idiot Boy, to something out of *Miami Vice*.

It was only the second gig I'd been to. I'd seen Lulu when I was a bit younger, about eIeven, I think, although I didn't actually see much of the concert as it was all standing and I was so little I kept getting pushed about. I spent the concert on the move, jumping up to get a glimpse of the stage. It was still a thrill and Lulu's voice was amazing, full of soul.

On the night of the Queen gig, me and Danny went up to Wembley and wangled our way in, probably with knocked off tickets, then walked right into a tout from Islington who had some dodgy VIP passes. I was a 'known' kid from the area and he probably also knew Danny's family but whatever it was, we were suddenly in the VIP enclosure. We had amazing seats close to the front. I really did believe I was something out of *Miami Vice*. Though to anyone taking a closer look, I was a bright red fourteen-year-old in someone else's sunglasses.

Queen were one of the best live bands ever. After that concert I was hooked, a massive fan. I still am. They played hit after hit and made the most extraordinary sound. Everything from the musicianship to the harmonies and the songs sent shivers up the spine. Danny loved it too.

Freddie Mercury was electric. I don't know if it's even possible to describe what an incredible performer he was. The moment I saw him coming on stage, I was completely gobsmacked. I had never seen or heard anything like it. It was the gig when he wore the famous yellow jacket. The whole thing blew me away.

That gig was a game-changer for me. I didn't know I was seeing one of the last concerts by one of the greatest performers that ever lived.

When me and Danny left Wembley Stadium that night it was as if we were stepping into a new world. One where everything was bigger and better. That was the Freddie Effect. Ordinary suburban streets seemed full of endless possibilities. We were on a high. An amazing, natural high, belting out Queen songs on the way to the tube station, part of a joyous crowd, everyone doing the same. All ages, all kinds of people, arm in arm, celebrating an incredible experience. All feeling the rush of shared happiness, what-ever ups and downs might have been going on in their lives. That's what the world would miss if we didn't have live performance. It can be such a force for good. At its best, it has an extraordinary power that stays with you forever.

When Freddie died, in late 1991, I was so sad. The sense of loss felt strangely personal. I was far from alone in feeling like that. His battle with AIDS had been kept secret from the public for as long as possible, to give him and those closest to him some privacy, and the outpouring of grief around the world from all those touched by his extraordinary talent was phenomenal.

In the international school, with everyone coming and going, friendships sometimes ended abruptly, without warning. You got to really like someone, they'd be there for a while and, just when you thought something was a bit settled in your life, their families carted them off somewhere else. There were no mobile phones, Facebook or internet, so when people left, that was it. Though some of us who met at the Southbank school did manage to get back in touch years later.

One of the best things about the school was the various trips and holidays we went on. I loved them. I think I had four holidays with the Southbank and they were all memorable. Filming *Revolution* had whetted my appetite for seeing parts of the world beyond Islington – and Tottenham. We went on three skiing holidays, two to Switzerland and one to Andorra. I took to skiing like a fish to water. I was a natural – I loved it. Pretty much the first day I was up on skis and off down the slopes and a few days later I was hitting jumps. (Many years later, in 2016, I made the highest jump of any amateur in the history of Channel 4's *The Jump*.)

It wasn't only skiing I got the chance to experience. Pretty much as soon as I started at that school we went to a kind of summer camp way out in the countryside where we slept in little wooden cabins. Growing up, I'd seen American kids go to camp in the movies and it was like another world to me – but now, suddenly, I was in it. It was like the movies had come to life.

On a day trip to France with the school I saw posters for *Revolution*. I popped into the cinema and to my surprise saw myself on the big screen dubbed into French. Back in London, as part of our history course, we all had to go and watch the film. There I was, on screen alongside legendary Hollywood actors. Up until then I'd not really spoken about it. It was quite nice feeling anonymous at school but that blew my cover.

19

Meeting Mario

WHILE I WAS AT THE SOUTHBANK SCHOOL WE'D MOVED
again, this time to Cockfosters where my aunt had bought
a house. We had been in Tottenham less than a year and
now I was catapulted into another area. The new neighbourhood was much more suburban than the one we'd
been used to. Streets full of identical 1930s semi-detached
houses, some Art Deco, others more Tudor style. Dull, you
might say, but nice, with a garage and a car parked outside
every house. If you close your eyes and imagine what a
typical road would look like in an outer London suburb,
it would be my street in Cockfosters. Big houses, lots of
trees, wide roads. It felt unusual to be somewhere so nice
and normal compared with our old neighbourhood. It was
a good area and family oriented. It still is.

We lived on a road called Sussex Way. I had a tiny bedroom at the front of the house. The hard thing – a really hard thing – was that for the first time it was me on my own with Aunt Carol and Mick. Scott, who was now sixteen, had begun having more rows and moved to live in a squat. Something had gone wrong with his relationship with Mick and they were constantly clashing. I was used to being the difficult one, so it felt strange and messed-up. The next thing I knew, Scott was away. I missed my brothers, even though they'd started leaving when I was just seven, after Mum died. First Mark, then Darren got sent to live somewhere else, although I still saw him a lot at school and stuff. Finally, Scott.

I was the last one left.

Me and Mick still didn't get along. As far as I was concerned, he wasn't a nice guy and made the atmosphere around the house tense and cold. It was like living with a control freak. There was minor stuff, like being told I couldn't watch certain TV programmes, like *EastEnders* or *Crimewatch*, even though I was fourteen years old. I found that level of control really hard to handle. 'No one fucking tells me what to do,' I thought. I'd be on my own in my little box room with a tiny portable television and they'd be listening at the door to check I wasn't watching anything I'd been told was off limits.

My friend Mario remembers walking in on me one time when Mick was slapping me really hard. Mario was shocked. For me, being slapped was normal, I was used to it, but Mario came from a different kind of family and

176

couldn't believe it. I tried to stand up for myself. I wasn't in the mood to take any shit anymore, not after everything I'd been through. I might have been getting walloped, properly walloped, but I used to say to him, 'You're not my dad.'

Meeting Mario was a lucky break. He and his family gave me everything I was missing at home, particularly now I lived that much further from the Wooders. He lived just a few doors down and we met after his dad did some work for my aunt and mentioned to Mario that I'd just moved in and he felt sorry for me because I was by myself. He suggested Mario call and say hi, so that's what he did. He walked down the road and knocked on the door. That was all it took. We're still friends.

He introduced me to his mates and suddenly I had a big group of local friends, most of whom Mario had known for a decade or so. Since I got on with him, there was a good chance I'd like his friends too.

Mario's house was a little bigger than ours and had some beautiful features, like a stained-glass Arts and Crafts-style window above the front door. The atmosphere there couldn't have been more different from my own house. While mine was as cold as you could get, Mario's was warm. Mario's dad loved having people round. He loved family, loved people being in the house. There were three kids: Mario was the youngest, his brother was a little bit older than him and then his sister was the oldest. When their dad got home from work they'd all sit down to eat together, like a proper family. I couldn't believe it, just as

Mario couldn't believe it when he saw me being hit by my aunt's partner. I was welcomed into his family and soon started sitting down to eat with them, too.

Maybe it made such an impact on me because it was so different from home. I remember it so well. There was a traditional Greek embroidery on the wall in the hallway, made by Mario's mum, and pictures of the family every-where, tons of them. I couldn't help comparing it with my own home. Mick was a bookie and had put photos and paintings of horses all over our walls. Their house is exactly the same now as it was when I was a teenager. I love that – I went back recently and was instantly surrounded by happy memories.

Downstairs at the back was a big dining room where everyone would sit around a huge table on leather captain's chairs – all moulded wood and really quite ornate. There was a 1970s smoked glass unit bursting with crockery and glasses – so many glasses! And there was every kind of cup you could ever imagine. I think they're all still there. There were beautiful little ornate Greek coffee cups, too. But for all the very many times I was at Mario's, no one actually used anything except for the whisky glasses. There was also a spare table they'd drag out so that more people could come in and eat and talk and hang out. Sometimes you'd get twenty or so people in that room – aunts, uncles, cousins – talking the night away. I was often the only one who wasn't part of the family but they were so kind to me I felt like I was. It felt like I'd walked into *My Big Fat Greek Wedding*!

The older generation would talk in Greek, others spoke English. It was a real mix. Mario's dad would sit at the head of the table by the windows, closest to the barbecue, as if he were king of it all. Whatever the season, whatever the weather, there would be a barbecue. And Mario's mum would be constantly in the kitchen. Mario still says that those were some of the liveliest, most fun periods of his life and I feel glad to have been a part of it.

Sometimes, the television would be on in the living room. That room was quite something, too. Just by the window there were two huge plinths with flowers on the top; there were proper Grecian columns either side of the television. We'd sit on the plush brown velvet sofas and watch the telly with Mario's dad. He had his favourite spot on the sofa, too – he was a creature of habit.

Funnily enough, he wasn't a fan of *EastEnders* and used to shout at the telly when it was on, although, ironically, it was the raised voices he was complaining about: 'They're always shouting – why are they always shouting?' he would yell. Years later, he did admit to being a fan of Ricky and Bianca. He said we brought more comedy to it – like a young version of Jack and Vera in *Coronation Street*.

I developed a real interest in Greek culture through Mario's family. The local Greek community was growing, a lot of families moving into Southgate, Cockfosters and Oakwood. There was quite a mix of Greek and Jewish people in the area. I was the odd one out. As always!

I couldn't get enough of Greek food. I'd watch Mario's mum make amazing dishes from scratch and became fascinated with cooking and interested in learning about food and flavours. Cooking was to become a big thing for me, and all this was part of the process.

At Aunt Carol's, Mick liked cooking and was good at it, which was unusual for a bloke back then. The food was almost always something British, well made with good ingredients. He'd do a great Sunday roast with all the trimmings, which was his signature dish. Steak pies and lamb chops were often on the menu. Nearly everything was classic meat and two veg. It wasn't ever anything 'out the box'. Even the most basic pasta and rice dishes were still considered exotic for working-class families then. No one would think of buying garlic or fresh parmesan – which for most people comprised something processed in a plastic tub. The smell was bad, like sick, until it melted into your spag bol, anyway. It came as a surprise when people went to an Italian restaurant for the first time to find that proper parmesan smells nothing like that.

When I wasn't with Mario's family, I started taking more interest in what Mick was doing in the kitchen. Cooking was one of the few things we could share without getting into a fight. It was therapeutic for both of us, I think. The best memories I have of him are from those times. He probably liked the fact I took a genuine interest. It didn't heal all our problems as they went far too deep on both sides but it was good to have more positive experiences.

The food at Mario's was all different and new to me. Mario and his brother and sister wanted fishfingers and chips but their mum would make black-eyed peas and I'd happily eat them straight out of the fridge. Everything tasted delicious. Mario couldn't understand it – he didn't even want to eat it when it was hot.

Most evenings, I'd eat at his house. There was something special about being introduced to totally new food by someone who knew what they were doing and Mario's mum was an amazing cook. There were dolmades – the stuffed vine leaves – and moussaka, and barbecued chicken with tzatziki sauce and potatoes. It wasn't as though I'd been to many restaurants or tasted much more than standard British food, so my introduction to Greek cuisine was like discovering a whole new world.

I even learnt about how to barbecue properly from watching his parents do it so many times. I saw the women prepare the meat and the men cook it. In the kitchen, the women would wash and chop and cut and stick meat on skewers and marinate it, and then outside at the barbecue the men would drink and argue about how much salt to throw on it! It seemed unfair on the women, who did most of the work, preparing everything else for the feast, including all the delicious Greek salad and dips and side dishes, that then the men would come in with the meat from the barbecue – the main event! – and get all the glory.

When I was fifteen I was asked to leave Southbank. It turns out I was considered a disruptive influence on all those posh rich kids. They were nice and calm and polite, and I was the one causing chaos. A letter arrived at Carol's asking very politely if I would fuck off out of their nice school forever. Classic. I was the only kid there paying school fees with money I'd earned myself and I was being thrown out. To be fair to them, I caused havoc. It was just daft pranks I was getting up to and showing off and routines and things. I'd stopped fighting, left that behind at my old school. But that was it – my time at the international school was over and I had to move on yet again. At least my new school, Southgate School, was near Carol and Mick's house so the early starts were a thing of the past, but I found myself in the middle of a whole new curriculum which was hard.

Apparently, one of the reasons Mario respected me was because I didn't try to impress him by telling him about any of the acting I'd done. And it was the same at my new school. It was something I didn't want to talk about. Secretly, I still had a thing about wanting to be in *Grange Hill*. In 1986, there had been a massive storyline about a character called Zammo, played by a mate of mine from drama school, Lee MacDonald. Zammo's addiction to heroin was totally gripping telly. Everyone was talking about it. When the show made an anti-drugs record, 'Just Say No', it caught the attention of America's First Lady, Nancy Reagan, who had launched a campaign in the States with the same name. Some of the *Grange Hill* cast were invited to Washington to meet her. It was unreal, seeing my mate on the TV news, on a sofa with the First Lady in the iconic White House. The fame that came with a hot TV show like *Grange Hill*, watched in millions of front rooms every week, was something else. I might have done a movie but I doubt if any of my new schoolmates had seen it – and even if they had, they would never have recognized me with long curly hair and my teeth blackened.

I was quite popular in my own right. For someone who'd come along at such a late age to the school when everyone was already quite tight I did pretty well. I made myself fit in. Maybe that's because I had to. I'd spent my whole life being a chameleon, learning to fit in with whoever I was with. Maybe my experience at the international school helped with that, too.

The only thing was, I found myself picking fights again, despite having vowed to put all that behind me. I'm not sure why. In my first week, I spotted the hardest kid in school and went for him over absolutely nothing. Maybe I thought he'd looked at me the wrong way. It was almost like some primal signal went off in my brain: I'm going to show you fuckers. Maybe because stuff wasn't great at home at that point or maybe because it was so ingrained in me that fighting was what you did. That was why it was so good for me to meet Mario and his family. They were respectable, not getting up to thieving and all the other bad stuff I knew. They were the right kind of influence.

We dated two girls who were best friends with each other. Mario dated Katie and I was with Melanie who, for my money, was the prettiest girl in the school. She lived in Winchmore Hill, which was one of the nicer areas. I don't know if it's true but I might have attracted Melanie's attention because I looked a bit out of the ordinary.

Everyone else looked 'clean' – shiny shoes, suburban and respectable – and all the same. I rocked up with my Doc Martens, my jeans rolled up, this trendy little army jacket. Mario thought I looked like a French exchange student. I suppose that went down quite well with the girls. It stood us in good stead.

I loved that army jacket. A long one with big buttons. I used to have a little cut-off one as well. I was into vintage clothes by now. I'd discovered a vintage shop in Covent Garden called Flip of Hollywood where I'd get my Levi's and army jackets. I was the first kid to wear cowboy boots in my area. I didn't care what anyone else thought. Sometimes I got a bit of grief, from piss-taking to bullying, but it never bothered me. I did my own thing. And anyway, the girls liked it.

So I'd arrive at school looking like I didn't have a care in the world. I'd come from all this trauma but I didn't tell anyone about it. That just wasn't something you did. I always used to say to Mario, 'You're such a worrier, you worry about everything!' I acted all 'go with the flow' – I guess that was what caught Melanie's attention!

We wanted to have fun. That was our main ambition. We were teenagers, so despite all the good food and nice people at Mario's house, we reached the point where we didn't spend much time there. Sometimes we'd be out and only come back when the food was ready, just in time to eat.

I was smoking then as well. Silk Cut, probably, because I used to nick them off my aunt, or the little Embassy ones. So we'd just hang about smoking. Well, Mario didn't smoke. We used to hang about at Oakwood Station, in Southgate, and in the McDonalds, of course. And I would sing everywhere we went – especially after a drink or two.

At Anna Scher's, we sang to warm up and I would dream of doing musical theatre, even though it wasn't her forte. I'd moved on from impersonating Elvis and now I was singing UB40 songs and the Drifters' 'Under the Boardwalk'. I got the Housemartins' 'Caravan of Love' spot on and people loved it. Singing in the style of someone else felt comfortable, like playing a character rather than being a singer, which I found scary. Strange when you think about it because years down the line I ended up on *Top of the Pops* performing my own hit single. I'm not sure if I had a premonition but just before I got the part on *EastEnders* I was singing the Bros song a lot – 'When Will I Be Famous?'

The only time Mario ever got kicked out of school was because of me. We were in history – me, Mario and our other friend, Laggy. I was picking my nose and flicking it at someone in front and he got up and said something to Mario, so he got up too. Next thing you know, there was a brawl. Mario was suspended.

It was a little bit disastrous for him. He had the kind of strict Greek parents who wouldn't let their children leave home until they were thirty-five, if they had the choice, and then all of a sudden he had to tell them he'd been excluded from school for fighting in class. Somehow they still thought I was a nice boy, although I wasn't always the best influence on their son.

One night, we went to a house party and I got into some bother and made my escape through a window. Mario was outside by the front door. The window opened, I jumped out, told him to run and we belted it down the road. There were about ten blokes chasing us but we managed to get away. The truth was I'd taken some cans of Skol from Mario's house and got him into drinking lager. I'd been drinking in the street before we went to the party so I was a bit wasted before we even got there – which probably explains how I found myself jumping out of a window with a pack of blokes on my tail.

I had an addictive personality but, thankfully, I wasn't really aware of drugs. I'd grown up streetwise with thieving and petty crime all around but there was no drugs culture in my circle. The worst I'd ever done was try to get high on Tipp-Ex. I knew from watching *Grange Hill* that there was nothing glamorous about hard drugs. The whole heroin thing was sick to me. At the same time, when I heard about weed, people smoking grass and getting high, I was intrigued. Other than cigarettes and alcohol, I was a complete innocent. I'd go to my local park, gather up dried leaves, crush them, roll them up and smoke them. I thought that was what 'grass' was. Some kids thought you could get high from smoking dried bananas. I never tried that.

The first time I smoked a proper joint it didn't agree with me at all. It sent me completely paranoid. My brain was just too young to handle it. Thank God I never smoked pot as a kid. It's not good when your brain is still developing. Now it's easier for kids to access drugs, to get hold of heavy-duty skunk and legal highs. You can get off your face and kill yourself from something bought over the counter. Cocaine's all over the fucking place, like it never used to be, and it's crap coke as well, cut with all kinds of stuff. We've all heard stories about people who've had a bad line or a bad acid tab. Bang, that's them gone, dead.

20

Back With My Brothers

I started petty thieving clothes again. Partly because I didn't have any money and partly because I was bored and messed up. I knew where that would lead but I didn't care. Although I'd passed my mocks at Southbank, I knew I wasn't going to pass my GCSEs at the new school and I didn't need them to be an actor anyway. So as soon as I turned sixteen, in January 1988, I left.

Carol and Mick didn't want me to carry on with the acting and were trying to get me to drop it all and find an office job. To be fair to them, they were probably just thinking this was the sensible thing to do, but to keep me away from acting was impossible and I would have been a total nightmare in an office or learning the ropes in a bank. Can you imagine sixteen-year-old me in a bank?! I was more used to bank robbers! I absolutely knew I had to give acting a chance. It was the only thing that seemed to really work for me, the only way to calm down my demons and my ADHD. I couldn't handle the idea of giving up.

Still, I'd drifted away from regularly going to Anna Scher's classes, which involved a long trek from Cockfosters, although I felt Anna was always there for me in the background. I was a bit low as well. I desperately wanted to act but I'd maybe lost my confidence a bit about getting roles. The last job I'd done was on the TV series *Crossbow* when I was fifteen. It was a sort of historical action adventure series, based on the tales of William Tell, who, legend has it, was forced to shoot an apple from his own son's head with a single crossbow bolt. The show involved lots of daredevil plots – all good swashbuckling stuff.

It was set in fourteenth-century Switzerland, but filmed on location in France. Surprise surprise, I was cast as a young urchin, so more scratchy costumes. Just fourteenth-century ones this time. I didn't have a main role or anything, but it was OK. It was always exciting to work on location. We got a nice hotel too, in Périgord, a lovely part of the Dordogne. It's a region I got to know very well in later life.

Anyway, me being me, things weren't going to run totally smoothly. Although this time it went wrong by me trying to do the right thing. Maybe I ate something that didn't agree with me, but whatever it was, I got this bad wind. Now, you don't want a bad dose of wind when you're filming and they're recording the sound, so I kept trying to hold it in. This wasn't a great plan either as I got tummy pains. I hoped they would just go away after sneaking off somewhere for a really good fart, but I think I'd held it in too long, so just when I thought everything was under control, I felt it brewing up again. Now I was at a table with everyone. I suddenly got up and tried to run away before I let rip what must now have brewed up into the world's biggest fart, but not quite soon enough.

The show was quite a big deal at the time, and over the run had stars like our own Brian Blessed and The Who front man and actor, Roger Daltrey. The American guest stars even included the brilliant actor and director Steve Buscemi and a very young Sarah Michelle Gellar, who was already a famous child actress. Despite the *Crossbow* part, I still felt I was in the wilderness a bit though, particularly after *Revolution*.

I was still friends with Dexter Fletcher and would go and visit him in Muswell Hill, sometimes at his mum's house or at his flat. He had his own place as he'd been in a lot of stuff since he was really young and had made decent money. Dexter is six years older than me but we'd hang out at his and watch the telly or play music, chat, all that. He encouraged me to keep at the acting, to find a way back in. Sandra Boyce and Dexter's mum, Wendy, who had kept an eye on me at Anna Scher's, had set up an agency, Fletcher & Boyce, when they left Anna's school. Through my friendship with Dexter, I got in with them again. They took me on and said they'd keep an ear to the ground in case anything came up that was right for me. I was always popping into their office to check up on things and generally pester the life out of them.

In early 1988, Sandra and Wendy were contacted by a casting director from *EastEnders* who said the show was looking to build a new family, one they wanted to be quite central to the drama, especially if they gelled and went down well with the public. They were looking for two teenage kids, a boy about sixteen and a younger sister.

Sandra and Wendy thought I could be a fit and set up an audition. By then I had started worrying that maybe no one would want me again. So when I heard I had an audition for *EastEnders* it almost knocked me off my feet.

I didn't tell Carol and Mick because I felt sure they wouldn't approve. I think Carol thought I had stopped all the acting stuff. I knew Mick was dead set against me wanting to act, constantly trying to steer me away from it, and that Carol would probably agree with him. I lied to Sandra and Wendy about not having told them at home what I was up to. They weren't aware that my legal guardians weren't fully on board. It wasn't their fault; I was good at hiding it. Somehow, I managed to keep the audition secret, which was amazing. I arranged for Sandra and Wendy to phone when no one was in.

On the morning of the first audition, my excitement was really building. I managed to scrabble around for loose change lying about the house for my train fare. Thankfully, as Mick was a bookie, there was always small change in corners and under sofa cushions. I scraped enough together to get me to Elstree, then to Islington afterwards to meet friends, and maybe get some chips or pie and mash.

At the first audition, they gave me a couple of pages of script and then I met the creators of *EastEnders*, Julia Smith and Tony Holland. Julia was also a director and producer and Tony Holland a writer. Also, there was producer/director Mike Gibbon.

I found out soon after it had gone well. Julia said they were looking for authenticity – actors who had a deep London connection and understood the people and the place, something she knew Anna Scher brought out in her pupils. Julia had already cast Susan Tully and Gillian Taylforth, also students from Anna's school. And there was good news – a second audition was on the cards.

When I got home, it wasn't exactly happy families. After the audition, I'd seen my girlfriend in Islington, hung about and then got the train back to Cockfosters at something like 9 p.m. I walked in the door and Mick started screaming at me, 'What time to do you fucking call this?' Something snapped inside me and I just turned my back and left.

I already knew I didn't want to be there any more but I think I was waiting for an excuse to leave. Now the moment had come I was calm, maybe too calm, as I walked along to Oakwood underground. I didn't have any money on me so I bunked the tube, which I usually did anyway. A lot of the stations didn't have barriers, and it wasn't hard to avoid the ticket inspectors in the carriages or at the other end of the journey.

I knew that Darren and Scott were living in a squat in Copenhagen Street, Islington, because I'd visited them, so that's where I headed. I turned up at their door and was welcomed in. No 'what are you doing here?' – they were happy to see me. Mark was still in contact with Carol and Mick so he acted as a kind of mediator and let them know where I was.

It was Darren who'd found the squat originally. He'd left his aunt to make it on his own a few years earlier. In the mid to late 1980s, you could find derelict flats and houses to squat in. Whoever owned them had maybe just left them lying empty, as renovating them would have been a massive job. Squatters would basically break in and change the locks. You could then legally squat there until whoever owned it went through a legal process to kick you out. Until then, you could even get an electricity supply connected up.

Sometimes the owner didn't give a shit about squatters or didn't find out their property was occupied for ages. There was a bit of an art to getting a decent place that more or less kept the wind and rain out. Bits of old cardboard boxes were good for blocking up smashed windows and carefully placed buckets under any leaky roofs came in handy when it rained. You could always get your hands on old mattresses and chairs and stuff. Darren had done well actually. Ours wasn't too bad at all.

It was a tiny top-floor flat in a crumbling Victorian building. You were better high up for a couple of reasons. Generally, there were fewer vermin. Ground floor squats could be bad for that and no one really enjoyed waking up with rats crawling around the bed. It was also considered more secure to be on the top floor. Even if you'd put decent locks on, there was a risk of being broken into, although anyone breaking into Darren's squat would not have come out of it well. It would have been a bit like when thieves broke into the home of Duncan 'Big Dunc' Ferguson, the legendary Everton striker. The newspaper reports went something like: 'Mr Ferguson apprehended the housebreakers, who were later taken to hospital, where they are expected to remain for some considerable time . . .'

We had one bed, a sofa and a telly in the corner. No pictures on the walls; it was about as bare and basic as can be. When you're living in a squat, possessions aren't important, all you want is your clothes. Since then, I've moved so many times and with each move the load gets bigger and bigger. So much stuff. Most people probably take more on holiday now than young people used to have moving into a squat.

We had a 'lounge', although that sounds a bit grand for what was basically the half of the room where the sofa was. The other half consisted of a few bashed-up kitchen units, a sink and an ancient cooker. Filthy but functioning. The bathroom wasn't somewhere you'd particularly spend any time, unless you were getting ready to go out and wanted to look sharp or had locked yourself inside for a quiet wank.

Our place wasn't in that bad a state. It was just very cramped. We slept one on the sofa, two in the bed. We often came in at different times, so it was a case of first come, first served. You slept wherever you could. There were so many arguments, though. We fought like cats and dogs at times, mainly me and Scott.

One time, I was on the little sofa, eating food off my lap and taking the piss out of him for something, when suddenly he grabbed my hair with both hands. It was fucking sore and I couldn't get out of his grip. I had a fork in my hand and stabbed him in the leg with it. It did the trick. He screamed and let go. When things got a bit too full-on, I'd go off and spend time back with the Wooders, but actually, especially at first, it meant something to be with my brothers. I'd not lived with Darren since Mum died.

Darren, being older than me and Scott, took charge. He was the dad, if you like. We were all into our food by then. Darren had done a bit of cheffing in a local pub. Scott too. They were both good cooks when they felt like it and were smart at getting meat and veg from the market and cooking up something nice. Standard British fare but it was tasty and I learned a lot. I'd already started getting interested in cooking after watching Mario's mum make all that amazing Greek food back in Cockfosters so this was just adding to my repertoire.

Darren did a mean spaghetti Bolognese and chilli con carne, as well as great sausage and mash with onion gravy. His Copenhagen Street squat speciality was a fry-up. He would make us full English breakfasts, though the word 'breakfast' is a bit misleading as they could appear at any time of the day or night. Scott and I would sometimes help out if we weren't too busy fighting but it was really Darren's thing. We didn't have a proper table or chairs so when we all ate together it would be the three of us squeezed onto the sofa, plates on our laps, watching the telly. We'd sometimes go for pie and mash at Manze's, which was still the same as when we were little kids running round the market.

We had a lot of laughs, the three of us, so it could be good, but it wasn't calm and the fighting had a kind of ripple effect. If me and Scott fought, Darren would take my side and have a go at Scott. It must have driven Scott mad as we were probably equally to blame for winding each other up. I was the baby brother, though, so Darren looked out for me. I totally milked this, of course. Any time I got in a fight with Scott, I was like 'I'm going to tell Darren,' because I knew that Darren would hit him.

Darren was such a good brother to both of us at that time. He was our rock. He had a big heart. A messed-up heart maybe, but basically he was good and totally loyal. Whatever he did, he had his own honour code and he stuck to it. He was proper staunch, as we'd say. Darren was still known for being a scrapper but was less wild than before. I think he saw it as his duty to look after us in the only way he knew how.

I had run away from Cockfosters with nothing but the clothes I was wearing. I was sixteen and hadn't organized any state benefits. My brothers looked after me – took me in and supported me. No questions asked. I was family. They didn't know I was going to get the job on *EastEnders*. They put a roof over my head when I had nothing, not knowing whether I'd ever have anything.

Mad as it was in a way, it was exciting, the three of us together again. And for me it was a taste of freedom. The only problem was I knew there was a danger I would slide back into my old ways. No one had an actual job. Darren and Scott were on the streets robbing. Same as ever. Petty thieving, trying to earn the meat. Nothing heavy. Mark, who was elsewhere and doing his own thing, was the more serious pro. If you went out and did whatever you did and came back with fifty quid, that was a good day. It was quite a lot of money back then.

Mark would come round to the squat sometimes, so for the first time since Mum died us four brothers were together again. I loved it. It was almost stable for a bit. About as stable as things ever got for us, anyway! We were home again, back in Islington, even if it was in a half-derelict old flat.

With some of the dosh Darren gave me, I went up west to get some new clobber sorted. I think he was hoping I'd get something normal-looking but he was in for a disappointment. I headed straight to my favourite shop: Flip of Hollywood, on Long Acre, in Covent Garden. Flip was about vintage and recycling, mostly 1950s and early 1960s Americana – alternative street fashion you could mix and match with other stuff. The shop had a musty smell, like a mix of mothballs and dust, from the racks and racks of old army jackets and overcoats that had been in wardrobes in the US for decades before ending up on a boat to London.

I spent what Darren gave me on a short-cut vintage American army coat, ripped Levi 501s and another pair of cowboy boots. I wore the boots every day, whatever else I had on. People would take the piss and laugh. Can't think why!

My brothers were into the typical Islington boy look back then: a new pair of Adidas Stan Smiths or Reebok classic trainers, freshly pressed Lacoste or Ralph Lauren shirt and perfectly ironed jeans. I would turn up looking like a cross between GI Joe and Buffalo Bill. But with Darren around, no one would dare mess with me, whatever I looked like. Or maybe people just accepted me. Islington was still where I was most at home.

In Chapel Market there was a big snooker hall where we used to hang out. I met a girl there called Coral, who was also sixteen and became my first real girlfriend. I'd dated girls at school but nothing serious and I was smitten. We'd hold hands and kiss, all quite soppy and romantic. She never invited me back to her house and I wasn't about to take her back to the squat. I kept it all private. I think I was quite shy, embarrassed in a way to introduce my first girlfriend to people, even the Wooders, although Maureen would have been lovely about it.

Coral was a popular girl that all the guys were after. She was pretty and funny and, for some weird reason, she liked me. She was a 'Brosette', a huge fan of Bros, and her love of the band was not to be messed with. She bought magazines for posters of her idols and wore her Doc Martens with old-style Grolsch beer bottle tops hooked on, just the way they did. The beer caps were the Bros equivalent of the Beastie Boys and their Volkswagen medallions, without teenage girls ripping badges off parked cars. One of the key fashion statements for any self-respecting Brosette was ripped jeans, the more ripped the better. In Coral's eyes, my taste for ripped jeans and cowboy boots was a bit Bros-like, even though the top half of my outfit was strict US 1950s military and didn't really fit with anything.

I introduced Coral to underground reggae and rare R&B stuff and she'd play me the stuff she liked, which wasn't just Bros. We'd spend ages hanging out, maybe find a quiet bench somewhere and share the headphones of our Walkman portable cassette players, sneaking kisses when no one was looking.

The famous Levi's 501 adverts of the time got so many young people into classic 1960s R&B and sparked a whole revival of some great old songs, ones I'd loved all my life, having heard them originally through my mum. The ads got me into Levi's, so I started searching for ripped-up originals. The four main adverts had storylines and the one Coral liked was about a teenage GI and his girlfriend parting at a railway station. He gives her his 501s, then she goes home, reads the letter he left in the back pocket of the jeans and puts them on. All to the soundtrack of Percy Sledge's 'When a Man Loves a Woman'. The ad was so fucking popular teenagers were waiting for it to come on TV. The song was re-released and climbed to number two in the charts and a whole thing started with girls wearing guys' 501s high on the waist with big belts. The girl in the ad was Rachel Robertson, who went on to act in films like *Mack the Knife* and *The Jungle Book*. A few years later, she married Nick Berry, who was to become a good friend of mine through *EastEnders*.

The great old soul songs in the Levi's ads might have proved timeless but when you're sixteen years old, relationships don't last. A month seemed like a long time and me and Coral kind of fizzled out. It was sweet, my first try at having a girlfriend. I think it was OK for her too. Scott was also seeing girls and Darren had started getting serious. By nineteen and a half he was with Nancy, a lovely girl. Not long after, they had kids.

Mark drove me up to Elstree for my second *EastEnders* audition. It was the same again, learning scripts in front of the directors, writers and producers. I wasn't working with the other potential cast members at that point, I was just running lines. Luckily that audition went well too and I got called back for the third one. At this point, I was starting to think that I might just actually get this. I was incredibly excited about it even if at the end of the day I still went back to a squat.

The third audition seemed to go well and I had a good feeling about it. Of course, I was nervous as fuck because I knew by then I was in with a really good chance and

I'd have been gutted going through it all and not getting the part. Even though it's something you've got to be hardened to as an actor. The casting process feels so ruthless when you don't get the part. Sometimes it happens over and over again.

After the third audition, I'd got myself so excited I kept going to the nearest phone box to ring Sandra and beg her to tell me if she had any news. I called every day at six o'clock without fail. We didn't have a phone at the squat so she couldn't call me.

Then I got the part and that was crazy exciting. I couldn't believe it. By 1988, *EastEnders* had been running for three years and was already a major drama. It had seemed to capture the public imagination through its brilliant writing and storylines that tried to deal with the social issues of the time.

My brothers were over the moon for me. I was so happy and grateful, even though at the same time I was thinking, 'Fuck. Now I've got to do the job – and keep it.' It was a bit daunting. One thing about our community was that everyone was thrilled to hear my news, going, 'He's one of ours.' There was a real sense of pride.

But then I was told there was a problem because I was still a minor and Sandra had to get herself to Cockfosters to get Carol, as my legal guardian, to say it was OK for me to do the job. She got a bit lost trying to find the house but once she did she persuaded Carol to give her permission. The documents were signed, and that was that.

21

EastEnders

My character was called Ricky Butcher. He was the son of Frank Butcher, played by Mike Reid, and he arrived on Albert Square when Frank became landlord of the Queen Victoria public house in spring 1988. Although I had turned sixteen, I was playing a fifteen-year-old. Sophie Lawrence played my younger sister, Diane.

My soon-to-be stepmum, Pat, a barmaid at the Queen Vic, was played by Pam St Clement, who had been in the show since 1986. Mike had already appeared playing Frank Butcher as a guest character in 1987 and had been so popular with the viewers that the producers had reintroduced him as a regular. I was totally in awe of him because I'd been a huge fan of the kids' gameshow *Runaround*, which he hosted. It was special to me because I'd watched it with my mum. Mike immediately took me under his wing and became a real father figure. A lot of the programme's storylines centred around the pub, as the hub of the local community, so the Queen Vic family were at the heart of much of the drama. The pub's occupants before us were 'Dirty' Den and Angie Watts, played by Leslie Grantham and Anita Dobson, and their family, who became TV icons, so we had huge boots to fill.

The very first scene I did was in that pub, the legendary Queen Vic, playing the fruit machine.

I remember being extremely nervous. That first day on set, all you're hoping for is to get your line out at the right time. It can be quite scary and it felt worse than usual because I knew it was such a big show. Thankfully, the producers and writers really eased us into it and made sure I wasn't given too much to do in the beginning.

Nick Berry played Simon 'Wicksy' Wicks, who became my character's step-brother when his mum Pat married my character's dad. Pat Butcher was an impressive figure. Wicksy was also a major character and Nick was the programme's first pin-up. He was one of the first British actors to become a pop star, when his single 'Every Loser Wins' spent three weeks at number one in the UK charts in 1986. It became the second-biggest selling single that year and won an Ivor Novello award.

Nick was such a lovely, modest guy. Right from the start he made me feel so welcome and sort of protected me. He was almost a decade older but the age gap was perfect in a way. He had experience in how to handle things but was also a great laugh and made it easy for us to become friends. As soon as he discovered I was living in a squat in Islington, quite close to the posher bit where he'd bought a flat, he offered to drive me up to work and back again. So that was the start of a new routine. Nick used to be really into classic cars and I'll never forget the first time he turned up outside the squat in a gleaming Jaguar E-Type, ready to drive me to work. We were both obsessed with music and sang along with whatever was on the radio most of the way to Elstree. He was a big star, a proper household name, and when we arrived at the gates to the studio there were hordes of fans waiting. As soon as they spotted him the screams went up: 'Wicksy!' 'Nick!' 'I love you, Nick!' The car was mobbed. Screaming girls waving banners and posters, begging for autographs. I had never seen anything like it. It was like Beatlemania or something. I watched, open-mouthed, thinking, 'Fucking hell!'

Mike Reid was so good to me and made everyone around him laugh. He was such a funny guy and took a shine to me straight away. I would ham up my lovably dim and dippy Ricky and he would shout, 'Rickaay!'. None of us knew just how much that would catch on, especially when it came from Patsy Palmer playing Bianca later.

Pam St Clement mothered me in a way. She was incredibly kind. Wendy Richard was kind to me as well – she was lovely. She'd been a very successful actress for a long time, starring in big shows for decades, like *Are You Being Served?*. She had grace and an air about her that could be intimidating. Some people were quite scared of her. If she liked you, you'd get the benefit of her wicked sense of humour but you wouldn't want to get on the wrong side of her.

I always got on well with June Brown, who played Dot Cotton. I was a big fan of hers and she used to tell me she enjoyed watching me act, seeing what I was bringing to the character. June was one of the funniest people I've ever worked with, every bit as sharp as you would expect.

They all gave me confidence. They'd say, 'That was really nicely played, you did well, son.' I needed to hear that! I was so young, I needed the boost – I think most people do. It makes a huge difference if actors you admire say you're doing well.

Years later, Nick said he could tell immediately that something was missing from my background. He was from a stable family himself and quickly understood it was the kind of thing I yearned for. It made him feel a bit more protective towards me when I was starting out on *EastEnders* and still very young. Another reason the cast were more protective than normal was because *EastEnders* actors suddenly got famous. So they did what they could to shield me. We became very tight-knit and close. I'd found a new family, with new mums and dads, in *EastEnders*. When I was older, I could reflect on how I had been made to feel welcome and I would try to do the same for other youngsters coming in, to help them find family in the cast and crew, just as I had.

They filmed the show in advance so I had five weeks of being anonymous, of still being me, before *EastEnders'* viewers would see me as Ricky Butcher. Five weeks of living in a rundown squat, knowing all the while that I was about to be on the telly in bloody *EastEnders*. It felt mad. As a sixteen-year-old, those five weeks seemed like a long time. At least I had some money, after living off my brothers. My wages were sent straight to Sandra and Wendy. They were very wise and told me I didn't need the full amount. They gave me an allowance of £200 a week and put the rest into a savings account for me. I used to get the bus to Stoke Newington every Friday to pick up my cash.

The first episode I was in was broadcast on 12 May 1988.

Since I'd got back to Islington, I was going around to the Wooders a lot. In fact, I first saw myself on screen at their house. The whole family gathered in front of the telly for the occasion. There was so much anticipation that night, everyone counting down to the programme coming on that you'd have thought we were about to watch a royal wedding or a moon landing or something! Then the famous *EastEnders'* theme started up. The atmosphere in the room was electric. After all the stuff I'd been through, there was a beautiful moment where we all sat, my brothers included, and watched me make my first appearance as Ricky Butcher. As soon as I appeared on screen, the cheers went up. None of us could quite believe it, especially me. There was my face on the TV in the corner of a room that had been a huge part of my life since my mum died. Now here I was, making my debut in one of TV's biggest dramas, with all the people I was closest to around me. We had quite a party that night, a proper celebration. Fancy drinks, sausage rolls and sandwiches, crisps and nuts in posh bowls.

My life was about to change completely, I just didn't know how yet.

22

Trying to Behave

I STARTED GETTING RECOGNIZED MORE AND MORE BUT LUCKILY
my fame hadn't spread far when I went abroad with some
mates. It was supposed to be a proper 18–30 type holiday
with some of the guys I grew up with, staying in one of the
huge apartment hotels in a resort on Tenerife. I was nowhere
near eighteen but I'd blagged my way in. Things seemed to
be shaping up nicely at first, as staying directly above us
was a group of girls, who we'd see wandering about in their
bikinis. One of them seemed to like me and would give me
these little looks and smiles. I was aching with lust and
pent-up testosterone, so this was almost too much to bear.
I was shy and insecure about all this stuff, as most youngsters are, but desperate to lose my virginity, just to find out
what that felt like as much as anything else.

One day it was just me and my mate Spencer in the apartment. We were leaning over the balcony, chatting to the girls and they invited us up. I was thinking, brilliant, this is it. Lovely jubbly. This could be the beginning of something great. I was nervous as hell but excited, too. So up we went and carried on chatting. Little did I know, the police were probably already on their way and I was about to be chucked into a fucking meat wagon for the second time in my life.

Five minutes later, there was a loud knock on the door. We opened up and it was the hotel security with about four police officers who immediately grabbed me and Spencer. We had no idea what was going on and started shouting. A guy across the hall, someone we'd never set eyes on before, came to see what the commotion was about so they arrested him as well. It turned out that while we were on our way up to the room from the floor below, one of the girls must have dropped a glass off their balcony. It had smashed onto the pool area, just missing some people on sun loungers. Of course, when the police barged in they assumed it must have been me and Spencer. You couldn't make it up. To think of all the shoplifting I'd done as a kid and never been caught. Here I was getting arrested in a properly terrifying way and I'd done nothing wrong.

We got taken to the police station, were fingerprinted, had our pictures taken and were banged up in a cell overnight. This was fucking Tenerife so it was piping hot. Because I was only in a pair of shorts, I kept sticking to the plastic mattress in the cell. More police came early the next morning and, wouldn't you know it, I was back in a meat wagon with Spencer, sirens going, handcuffed to the seats and taken to a little prison about fifty miles away. We were put in the most disgusting cell imaginable, with blood and shit all over the walls.

They gave us a packet of biscuits, Carnation milk and a plastic container of water. Those were our supplies to last all weekend. Turned out, you really didn't want to get arrested on a Friday in that part of the world back then because nothing was going to happen until Monday morning when the police came back. Spencer told them, 'We haven't done anything,' but every time he opened his mouth he got whacked with a baton, so I just thought, fuck it, I'm not going to say a word.

We ended up getting dragged to court, done for criminal damage and resisting arrest, and given a fine. I was still in just my shorts when I appeared in the court – no top on. When they finally said we could go, they couldn't get my handcuffs off. The bloody things were jammed. The policeman who spoke the best English started joking about firing at the cuffs to break them open. He kept saying, 'You hold up and we shoot!' half serious and laughing as well. I was genuinely scared.

In the end they had to take me to a scrap yard, put my hands in a vice and saw the cuffs off. Then we got taken to the British Consulate and put on a plane back to London. After all that, I was still very much a virgin . . .

Happy holidays! The one stroke of luck was that the news-papers never found out about it.

Spencer was one of my best mates but, sadly, he devel-oped a serious drug problem and, tragically, died very young.

I was trying my best to behave on set and resist most temptations not to, which was very unusual for me. I was so desperate to be accepted and not fuck up. The first real bit of trouble I got into was a surprise as I genuinely didn't think I had done anything bad.

Viewers may remember the milk float that appears in *EastEnders*. It's part of the landscape, involved in the odd scene, trundling past in the background first thing in the morning. One day, I had a break during some scenes and went for a wander on set. I laid eyes on the milk float and thought I'd have a sit in it. Then I realized I could start up the electric motor. It was parked up a back lot and no one was around so I decided to take it for a spin, thinking that would be OK. I went for a joy ride around the whole of Elstree's outdoor studios, a huge area. I was in a world of my own, happy as a pig in shit, memories flooding back of the golf buggy escapades in Florida with Danny. Some of the lots were empty but you might think that anyone who saw a teenager driving a milk float in the middle of the day would find it a bit odd and stop me. To my amazement, nobody did.

It was so exciting to drive a vehicle. Any vehicle. Even a moped was a thrill. It may not have been Nick's E-Type Jag but taking the famous Albert Square milk float for a spin at top speed – which, in fairness, was not fast at all – still seemed wildly exciting.

After what seemed like not that long a time, I casually drove back to find the crew director and producers freaking out. They had been looking for me as I was due on set. I got a serious telling off. A verbal warning. That was when it dawned that I was working in a serious environment and couldn't do crazy stuff.

My jaunt on the milk float soon became a running joke with everyone. When I went to do my next scene, word spread and there were howls of laughter. For ages afterwards I couldn't walk past the milk float without some gag or other being cracked or someone humming a few bars from Benny Hill's novelty hit 'Ernie (The Fastest Milkman in the West)'. You can imagine the kind of stick I got.

23

Becoming Ricky

As the weeks went by, the attention that being in *EastEnders* brought almost knocked me for six. It always seemed glamorous when it happened to other people but when it happened to me, I wasn't sure how I felt. It was enjoyable sometimes but it could also be uncomfortable and weird. Luckily, I was prepared a little bit, which was largely down to Nick and his friendship. He did what he could to guide me.

I started to get more and more press coverage. Not only was I on telly, my face was on newsstands and magazine racks. My first big photo shoots were for teen magazines like *Mizz* and *Just Seventeen*, as well as various pop and pop culture mags. I'd find myself in hair and make-up, styled to within an inch of my life, turned into a pin-up on a poster. This was me now. My life had changed, although I hadn't yet become properly famous.

Then something even more strange happened. One of the world's top model agencies, Elite, approached my agents, keen to get me on their books. I seemed to be flavour of the month and Sandra and Wendy probably thought the publicity would be good. The next thing I knew, I was working with the celebrated photographer Terry O'Neill, who'd taken photos of everyone from Hollywood stars to royalty and US presidents. The pictures were for 'my book' to show casting agents. The money was crazy – I was told I could earn ten grand a day for advertising work. Then it all came to a stop. My BBC contract meant that I wasn't allowed to directly advertise anything. If I wanted to flog jeans or be the working-class face of some new campaign it would have meant leaving *EastEnders*. Acting was what I wanted to do so it was an easy decision.

Being part of a drama series like *EastEnders* was intense. The busy schedule meant juggling different episodes at the same time, which took some getting used to. I talked it through with Nick recently and we marvelled at how fast everything was, from learning lines to shooting scenes. He told me, 'The most overwhelming thing I remember was because there were only two episodes a week then, there were split filming days. So on a Friday, for example, there would be an outdoor shoot so you'd film scenes for two episodes. Saturday was a rehearsal for the following week's studio shoot. Basically, you had six scripts in your head at any one time.'

He was right. It was a lot to keep up with! You got used to it, although, as he said, the pace of things was bamboozling at first. No matter how welcoming and supportive everyone was you had to be up to speed because there was no time for second takes, no time to question your motivation.

If you've watched *EastEnders*, you'll know it's a show that constantly investigates family dynamics. When I arrived, with what Nick called my 'charm and cheek', the producers were keen to explore what it was like to be part of a modern blended family, as there were more and more of those in society. Well, families didn't come more blended than my own! So that was something I could easily understand.

Sophie, who played my younger sister, Diane, had trained at Sylvia Young's school, which focused more on musical theatre than we had at Anna Scher. Our dynamic worked well, although there was quite a contrast between us and our different ways of approaching our roles. Mike Reid came from a comedic background and Pam St Clement had masses of experience in theatre, television and film. Nick was also Sylvia Young-trained with roles in TV, film and on the stage under his belt. He already knew Sophie before she joined the *EastEnders* cast. It was a blend of different ideas and thoughts on how these actors would work together to make their characters come alive, gel and evolve.

In our blended family, the father ran the pub and lived in the flat above the premises with his kids. He fell for the barmaid, a tough character and hard on the outside with a bit of a dark past and a difficult relationship with her son. The two families were thrown together in a working and living environment that was claustrophobic and the storyline was built around how they dealt with it. How do they gel and grow as a family?

Later on, the storylines got more complex as Ricky interacted with more people. I'm probably best known for Ricky's relationship with Bianca. Patsy Palmer and I already knew each other before she joined the cast – she was at Anna Scher, too, and her brother knew my brothers. The feeling of family with her was very real and the on-screen chemistry was a result of that.

The writing on the show was brilliant. It tackled all the big issues of the time – racism, homophobia, poverty, illness. It was the first show to deal seriously with the AIDS epidemic, when Mark Fowler, Todd Carty's character, was diagnosed as HIV positive. The storyline unfolded over many years and, throughout, the Terrence Higgins Trust – the HIV and sexual health charity – worked with the production team to get it right.

EastEnders played an important role representing all kinds of issues in a way that would increase understanding and compassion, and it became the number one show in the UK with massive audiences – up to thirty million people watching per episode. It's difficult to get across today just how big and influential a show it was.

It meant there was a big responsibility on all of us to make everything work.

When it came to the Butchers, because the previous family in charge of the Queen Vic had been so iconic, there was work to be done to capture the public imagination. I think we all knew that humour was going to be important. Sometimes *EastEnders* was accused of being quite angry and serious with all the heavy storylines, so I think they hoped we would bring some good laughs.

Even at sixteen I knew how a long-running TV drama worked. If the cast and crew took to the actor playing the role and the audience took to the character they played, they would start getting more storylines. If it wasn't working, they would get eased out. It kept the actors on their toes. Most of us were on short contracts to start with, maybe a three-month option or, if you were lucky, six months, to see if the audience liked you, if you fitted in with the team. At the beginning it was pretty nerve-racking and all I wanted to do was get in there and get the work done. People were kind but at the same time everyone was busy. It was like a big well-oiled machine and I had to slot in. If I felt myself start to lose focus, I would think about what Sandra and Wendy had said: 'Basically, it's a trial. If you work hard and if they decide they like you, they may extend your stay.'

I had no idea how my character would develop. Would people like Ricky? Would they like how I played him? I started thinking, if they didn't like him, did that mean they didn't like me? I knew I had to stop worrying and just get my head down and keep focusing. Maybe the ADHD side of me wasn't such a bad thing because I had bursts of creative energy where things would work.

Julia Smith, one of the creators, was very much about not only how things came across on screen but how they work off screen too. When you're working under pressure at the sort of speed a show like *EastEnders* demands, you need people who are going to turn up, know their lines, do their scenes and add a lot to the production. Luckily, I did seem to fit in and, after a while, my new home on the show became more permanent. I could be creative but I also knew I had to work hard: I had to learn the lines, I had to be disciplined, wake up on time and turn up on time. Make sure I didn't look too much of a state when I arrived on set.

I started to stay with the Wooders more often when I needed to be in a calm environment. It was good to be around people who kept normal working hours. It helped me get into a routine and find a quiet space to learn my lines and focus. I was determined not to fuck things up. I knew how many other people would have loved to have the opportunity I'd been given and I was enormously grateful. I never let myself forget that. It was such a big thing and so huge in popular culture – strangely, even more so than a film, because a series like *EastEnders* weaved in and out of the lives of its audience, often for years.

I was so happy to be performing; it made me feel confident again and I knew it was the right thing for me. I was soaking up everything around me and finding a way to put it into my work. If I did a good scene, I could feel I was being helped and guided. Not only by the people I was acting with in that moment – like Mike, or Pam, or Nick – but other actors on set would make a fuss, tell me I'd done well. Their kindness meant a lot. It made me feel that I was accepted into their family and that I belonged there.

Although I was appearing in magazines and being recognized, it all felt new and surreal. I was more concerned with making sure I didn't fuck things up at work than being famous and tended to stick to my local area where people knew me and treated me the way they always had. There were a few who watched the show and were different with me and I suppose I could have milked it but I didn't. The whole fame thing hadn't really sunk in.

It only properly hit me one day after I'd been on a break and returned to work. I was raring to get back on set again. I'd learned my lines and the scenes were playing out in my head. In the meantime, more and more of the Butchers' storylines had been airing and it seemed like my role was starting to be a proper part of the show. Like most TV and film actors, I was in a kind of parallel universe, concentrating on the scenes I was about to do, rather than the ones I'd filmed five weeks earlier.

On my first day back, Nick came to pick me up. I'd sorted new mix tapes for him to listen to on the drive in. He'd got some new stuff too so we were singing and chatting away. I was thinking about my scenes, hoping they'd go well and looking forward to catching up with the cast and production team. Nick was grinning, telling me I'd been going down well with everyone. He didn't go into detail so we put on another mix tape and started talking music again.

As we approached the studio, I could see fans waving banners and posters. We drove up and they all started shouting for Nick as usual. The next thing I heard was some of the girls screaming, 'Look! It's him! It's Ricky!'

A crowd clustered round my side of the car. Nick lowered his window to sign stuff and the fans went crazy. I opened my window and things went equally berserk.

'Ricky!'

'Ricky!'

'Can I have an autograph?'

'Ricky, I love you!'

'Rickaaaaay!'

Nick leaned over and, with a big smile, he said, 'Welcome to the madness.'

Epilogue

I OWE A LOT TO *EastEnders*, THOUGH IT CAN BE A BIT overwhelming being in millions of people's living rooms twice a week, and even getting recognized outside of the UK. At least I was playing a character people liked, which meant I got a lot more warmth than hostility. Some of my character's storylines were central to some of TV's highest ratings – not only in the history of *EastEnders*, but in terms of all UK drama. When Ricky and Bianca got married in April 1997, that episode alone got over twenty-two million viewers. The numbers were mind-boggling to me.

As I said, *EastEnders* gave me a real sense of family. The whole thing, cast and crew, was a team effort. The actors weren't just thinking of themselves and their own roles, they were conscious of ensuring the other actors could make the most out of theirs. As much as you might think actors are paid to dress up and show off, there is also a giving side – the best actors are incredibly generous to work with.

For the first couple of years I was in the show I was still basically itinerant. I lived in two or three different squats that Darren managed to find before he and Nancy finally got their own place from the council. I'd still sometimes stay with the Wooders or with Nick Berry – the Berrys were now added to my list of surrogate families. They'd all advised me to get enough money in the bank for a deposit on my own place, and would look out for me till then. In a way, it was also good not to be on my own. Most people my age would be living with their own parents.

My earnings weren't that high during the first years, so I had wait a while to save up. I was still really young, so the Wooders and Wendy and Sandra helped me with all the paperwork and finding the right place, right by them and Nick. I bought a flat on Offord Road, which is just off the Caledonian Road, for eighty-five grand. That was an amazing feeling, to own my own place at the age of eighteen.

Nick would pick me up from Offord Road and drive me to the studio in one of his beautiful classic cars. My brothers were still all Islington-based back then too. Darren and Scott sometimes used to stay with me. Mark would come round. Things would still get heated between us all from time to time, but the love and loyalty was always there. I knew we'd all come through the same shit, so I knew how hard things had been for them as well. I felt very lucky I was being given this chance though the acting.

When you get famous, it can feel like suddenly everyone wants to know you. It was overwhelming and hard to tell whether the new people I met were only interested because I was on the telly. I also never knew how long any success I had was going to last. No actor ever really does, and you don't know who's going to be there for you if it stops. Not everyone has your back and will always be there for you. With my brothers and the likes of the Wooders and the Berrys I never had any doubt. We have stuck together through thick and thin. My career has included roles like Donnie Kimber in the award-winning drama series *Bad Girls*, presenting factual programmes, and appearing on huge shows like *Strictly Come Dancing*. I even had a bit of musical success, a restaurant in France and was a *Celebrity Masterchef* finalist. I've also had periods of feeling like I was in the wilderness. I realize for many people I'll always be Ricky, so thankfully it's a character I genuinely like, even if he's not always been the sharpest tool in the box.

When I started to become well-known, my dad suddenly reappeared and started leaving messages with my agents. I really didn't want to see him – even the thought of him brought back horrible memories. It was a very strange feeling, though, thinking of him being out there somewhere. I nearly did meet him one time. There was an arrangement that he'd wait for me in a pub. As I got closer to it I thought, 'no, I can't do it'. The whole thing was completely freaking me out. I'd already been warned that he'd only want to see me for the wrong reasons. He'd never made any attempts to get in touch before I was on the telly.

Curiosity killed the cat in one way, though. Even though I was sure I wasn't going to speak to him by the time I reached the pub, I sneaked a look round the door to see if I could recognise him after all these years, and if he still had hair.

I only found out a lot later that male pattern baldness comes through the mother's side.

If you've only known chaos, it's actually very difficult not to end up living a chaotic life. It's the thing that's familiar, so you tend to fall back into it without even realizing what you're doing. *EastEnders* brought structure to my chaos.

Losing my mum when I was so young and having a dad who wasn't in my life meant that I found the properly loving family I craved in other places, adopting other peoples' mums and dads along the way. Looking back, I can see that Carol had tried to love me, and tried to create something that clicked but, sadly, it just didn't work out. I could feel it, and she and Mick could too. That was why I was drawn to families like the Wooders, where somehow my love me or loathe me way of being seemed to fit. I am so lucky to still have them in my life, along with Mario and his parents, and Nick and his family.

After my own experiences, I know for sure that love and acceptance doesn't need to come in a conventional way.

You can find it among close friends, among people you work with, in so many other ways. I want everyone to know that if you're looking for these things you can find them. Don't give up hope or ever think that you aren't worth it.

Acknowledgements

Without the talents, dedication and hard work of my collaborator Martin Gray, Gordon Wise at Curtis Brown, commissioning editor Ingrid Connell and all at Pan Macmillan, this book simply wouldn't have happened.

Many other people were a big help along the way, often filling gaps and jogging memories.

My love and heartfelt thanks for help and allowing what felt like an important, but sometimes difficult story to be told, go my family; especially my brothers, Mark, Darren and Scott; Darren's children, Jodie, Danny, Alfie, Albie and Aura and Scott's wife Zoe and their children, Ruby and Nellie. Other family and friends who deserve a special thank you for their support and contributions include: the

Wooders: Danny senior and Maureen, Jackie, Pauline, Debbie, Joanne and of course Danny. Mario Savva and family; Maggie Diamond and cousins; Sharon Harris; Sallyann Sexton; the Freeds; John, Stuart, Margaret and the Evans family; Carole Mackie and Maggie. Others who have helped include Adrian Buchart, the incomparable Erik; Farber; Lisa Gow; Ellen Gray; and Gill Barker. A great support network of friends, includes, as ever, one of my closest ever, Simon Konecki, as well as Jeff Lim; Jeff Taylor; Nancy Gray; Paul and Sue Murphy; the Puds and the Bronsons.

As well as Martin, others who have worked alongside or helped in my career also became true friends, often along with their families. Among these are Nick Berry; Sandra Boyce and Wendy Fletcher; Wendy's son Dexter Fletcher; Patsy Palmer, the wonderful June Brown and all the great actors and broadcasters I've worked with down many years. Huge gratitude goes to Carolyn Weinstein; Julia Smith; Tony Holland; Mike Gibbon; the rest of the brilliant EastEnders production team and of course, the great Anna Scher who means so much to so many like me.

My own final thanks, from my heart, to Victoria Shores.

Hopefully the above has covered all the cast and crew, but just in case I missed someone I really do want to thank all those who have put up with me, supported me and been there for me through thick and thin.

Photo Credits